LONGMAN GROUP LIMITED
*Longman House,*
*Burnt Mill, Harlow, Essex CM20 2JE, England*
*and Associated Companies throughout the world.*

First published 1984
Twelfth impression 1994

Set in 10/11pt Baskerville, Linotron 202

Produced through Longman Malaysia, VP

ISBN 0 582 22389 X

# Contents

# Introduction: In conversation with Jack Rosenthal

*Where do you get your ideas from?*

Ask a straight question and, I'm afraid, you get two fairly devious answers. One is that I get ideas from 'nowhere' (which, I suppose, means my own experiences), and the other is I get them from 'everywhere' (i.e. other people's). The first includes the substantially autobiographical plays like *P'tang Yang Kipperbang*, and the second covers the rest, which, although fictional, are based on either real people, or actual events.

I like to find incongruity in characters, apparent paradoxes, eccentricities. And since I believe that all of us are walking examples of those characteristics, then almost anyone I meet could be fodder for 'fictionalising'.

I also like to find ideas in the minutiae of specialised areas of working life. The day-to-day mechanics (and inbuilt dramas) of jobs that we all know of, but know very little about: a registrar of births, marriages and deaths in *Well, Thank You, Thursday*, taxi-driving in *The Knowledge*, a film unit in *Ready When You Are, Mr McGill*, a returning officer in *Mr Ellis Versus the People*

*So you start with the situation?*

Normally I prefer to 'feel' the character first, then think of a story which will serve as a framework for exploring that character. But, often, it happens the other way round. In *Well, Thank You, Thursday*, for example, it occurred to me that a Register Office might offer a treasure trove of material for the kind of play I like to write. You go to a Register Office on one of the most emotionally-charged days of your life: either to 'name' your newly-born child, or to get married, or to document the death of a loved one. But, to a Registrar, it's just another day. To me it's dramatically interesting, if, in the midst of all the 'significance' with which her customers imbue the day, the Registrar herself is preoccupied with something which, to us, is utterly mundane, but, to her, is of immense importance. In this case, the delivery of her new desk.

## How much has your childhood influenced you as a writer?

Almost completely, as it always does whatever you do in life.
The obvious experiences – Mancunian, Jewish, poor, bombed in
the war – I wrote about in *The Evacuees*. The later ones –
grammar school, adolescent passions, growing up emotionally –
I wrote about in *P'tang, Yang, Kipperbang*. Growing up
intellectually, I wrote about in *Bar Mitzvah Boy*, although the
play wasn't autobiographical (other than in feeling . . . a sort of
wish-fulfilment in hindsight).

I say they're the obvious ones because, as we all know,
childhood experiences colour what we think and feel about
almost everything from then on. Very occasionally as an adult
you learn to change long-held opinions or modify deeply-felt
feelings; and I think you deserve a pat on the back when that
happens. Maturity, I believe, means being aware that you
haven't yet reached it. These experiences help to give us our
own individual characters. And therefore, if you become a
writer, they largely dictate not only what you write about, but
also how you write it. It's often said that, however many plays a
playwright writes, they're all the same play in the end. We all
have our favourite hobby-horses, and our personal instinctive
way of riding them. Not that it's deliberate. The stories,
characters and settings may be entirely different; but the
underlying *feeling* or preoccupation is often the same. Even (to
my horror, when I re-read plays of mine) in actual words of
dialogue.

## What's your hobby-horse then?

It's difficult and a little inhibiting to say what feelings and
attitudes are in my own plays. I'd rather the audience spotted
them. Articulating them myself makes me a bit scared of
starting the next play. But, here's a tentative, over-simplified
stab at it. Forgive me if it sounds pretentious . . .

We live in a world that's tough, bitterly unfair, cruel,
indifferent, *inhuman*. Yet it's humans who people it. We're all
biologically the same: the regulation couple of ears each, five
toes per foot, etc. We all have the same physical feelings; we all
sneeze, eat and sleep, get pins and needles. Emotionally, we all
have the same urges, and needs, and fears, and dreams and
nightmares.

So far, so good: we all seem relatively human. The trouble

seems to start when we then do one of two things ... both extremes. On the one hand, we either completely forget that other people are like us; or, on the other hand, we find it impossible to understand that living their own lives has made them not *precisely* like us. (In *P'tang, Yang, Kipperbang*, for example, Alan finds it intolerable that Geoffrey fancies Ann like *he* does, and intolerable that Shaz and Abbo *don't*.) We either completely forget that pain hurts others as it hurts us, or find it impossible to understand that they may like egg and chips when we like fish and chips. When we completely forget our similarity or find it impossible to understand our dissimilarity (ranging from what dinner we want to what government we want) we've got our inhuman world of humans. And that self-contradiction makes tragi-comedians of us all.

People made (internally) lonely by the unconcern of others (who are equally lonely) is what interests me; like Mr Ellis in *Mr Ellis Versus the People*, and his wife, and his two helpers. Characters, I hope, we can identify with and sympathise with, surrounded by indifference and incomprehension. Maybe that's the result of a childhood in which, although I was unstintingly loved, I bit my nails watching those around me tear themselves and each other to pieces. I still bite them now.

### How did you begin as a writer?

The first thing I did was my life story. Since I was nine at the time, it was only three-quarters of a page long. When I was eleven I wrote a radio sketch for Suzette Tarri, a comedienne who was famous in those days. I sent it to the BBC, and the BBC returned it. In my early twenties, I adapted James Joyce's stage-play *Exiles*, changing its locale from Ireland to England. The BBC returned it, with one criticism: that I'd changed it from Ireland to England.

My next attempt met with success ... and, as almost always, there was an element of luck that helped. I was working at Granada Television, in its very early days, as a promotion writer – that's the person who writes brief snatches of material about the evening's forthcoming programmes for the announcers to read. After a year or two, I left to join an advertising agency to write commercials, and the man who took my place was Tony Warren – the creator of *Coronation Street*. Out of interest in Tony's talent, I watched the first few episodes and felt that *his* street was right up *my* street. I rang him and his producer, Harry Kershaw, to ask if I could be given a chance to write a trial script. They said yes; and, after I'd delivered it, I was commissioned to write Episode 30. I went on to write another one hundred-and-fifty episodes.

In between these, I began to write episodes of comedy series and drama series and eventually my own comedy series. Finally, I devoted all my writing to plays and films.

### What do you aim to achieve in your plays?

Now there's a conversation-stopper if ever there was one.

Well, I suppose, not really deliberately, not always consciously even, I want to make people aware of the loneliness in others. They're well aware of it in themselves. James Joyce wrote of 'the soul's incurable loneliness'. Well, I think if we shout about it loudly enough, we may, in however small a way, in however small a circle, begin to *find* a cure.

In *Polly Put the Kettle On*, the principal character uses the entire drama going on around her in order to live out her own. She's alone. No one listens to what she's *really* saying, to what she's really *meaning*. Not many people in my plays do listen. They're already – like most of us in life – using the time when other people are speaking to work out *their* next thought.

When we have our initial read-through with the actors in my plays, I always point out to them that their character should never listen to the others. I want the audience to see it's wrong, to feel the loneliness it causes. If we really *listen*, we'll *understand*. And, if we do, the person we're understanding will be that much less lonely. And we'll have started being human.

Perhaps my most important aim of all is to do this while making my audience laugh. Because then they're laughing at themselves. I believe comedy is the best way to learn the truth about ourselves. Maybe it's no accident that human beings are the only animals that laugh . . .

P'tang,
Yang,
Kipperbang

## The Cast

Alan
Ann
Geoffrey
Abbo
Shaz
First boy
Second boy
Third boy
Eunice
First girl
Second girl
Majorie
John Arlott, *in voice-over sequences*
Alan's mother *always out of sight*
Proprietor of fish and chip shop
Two workmen
Tommy
Miss Land
Headmaster
Gym teacher
French teacher
Botany teacher
Policeman

# P'tang, Yang, Kipperbang

## 1 A dream sequence

*The play opens to slow motion action from the 1948 England v. Australia Test Matches, strangely and unrealistically coloured. Snatches of John Arlott commentary are heard.*

JOHN A   Good morning to you from Lords, and the second England-Australia Test Match of 1948.

    The umpires are out ... and the England fieldsmen. And here are Barnes and Morris for Australia, out to the wicket to bat.

*A 14-year-old schoolgirl in close-up. The close-up gradually tightens. Her eyes are yearning. Her lips are shaped in a half-sad, half-excited smile. The smile fades: her lips are now preparing to kiss.*

    *More cricket, as above, building to a climax.*

    *A 14-year-old schoolboy in close-up. His face is solemn, belying the intensifying drumming of his heart-beats. His dry lips part slightly. It's now about to happen ... the long longed-for kiss.*

    *More cricket, as above, nearing its climax.*

    *Shot of the boy and girl in close-up. Very slowly, tenderly, reverently, gravely, they're about to kiss. In awe and wonder ... like the first kiss of Adam and Eve.*

    *As their lips are about to touch, we hear –*

MOTHER   Alan! Ten past eight! What are you doing up there!

*A shot of three cricket stumps – as they're hit and shattered by a cricket ball.*

    *The shot of the boy and girl shatters into pieces.*

## 2 Alan's bedroom (morning)

*Alan is lying in a dishevelled bed. He wakes up, opens his eyes and blankly takes in his familiar surroundings ... a couple of sporting pictures, a framed copy of the News of the World's Victory Cartoon (1945), a cricket bat, a football, roller skates, a violin and music stand. His hair's a little matted, his heart still thudding from his dream.*

MOTHER  Will you try this morning, Alan? Something. Anything. A lightly boiled egg.

ALAN  Please God, let it be today. Somehow let it come true today.

MOTHER  A few cornflakes wouldn't hurt you . . .

ALAN  I know Thursdays are difficult for you, what with the girls having double Domestic Science while we're on double P.T. But if just somehow. I don't think I can last out another day.

MOTHER  If I made you fresh air on toast, would you eat the toast?

ALAN  And, in return, I promise . . . I hereby solemnly promise that I won't even think about . . . *try* not to even think about . . . the *other* things. I didn't all day yesterday, or last night when I got in bed, and I'm not now. I'm not, honest to God, God. (*He takes his hands out from beneath the bedclothes to prove it, and lays them on the counterpane*) Look – no hands. And if I catch the school bus, I'll *stand*. Then even when it bumps up and down it won't start me off. It's only when I'm *sitting* that it . . . Anyway, I'm too late for the school bus. I'll have to run to school. And it hardly ever does it when I'm running. (*The tears now fill his eyes*) Please God. Today or tomorrow. Or early week at the latest, weather permitting. Just one kiss. One'll do. And I'll never ask for anything again.

## 3 Outside a modest terraced house (day)

*Alan emerges from the front door – a hurriedly-dressed figure in worn, rumpled grammar school uniform. Slung over his shoulder is a bulging, tattered satchel; and under one arm is a white, rolled-up towel with gym vest, pants and shoes inside it.*

*His face is now brightly scrubbed. His school cap sticks out of his pocket. As he closes the door behind him –*

MOTHER  Have you got your towel for P.T.?

ALAN  No answer was the stern reply.

*As he's about to close the door again –*

MOTHER And your vest and shorts?

ALAN Mother. I'm fourteen!

*As he's about to close the door yet again –*

MOTHER A pound to a penny you didn't blanco your pumps.

*Alan throws a defeated glance at his dirty gym shoes sticking out of the towel.*

MOTHER And, for God's sake, work up an appetite! Force yourself.

*He closes the door, and walks off at a brisk pace down the street. As he does so –*

JOHN A Bedser then, snatches the ball out of the air from Evans's throw ... polishes it on that not inconsiderable chest of his and prepares, this giant of a man, to bowl yet again to Don Bradman. With Bradman 63 and Australia a dismaying 235 for 1, here ... (*Alan starts running.*) ... he comes. Gathering pace, gathering strength, pounding ... (*Alan runs faster.*) ... pounding powerfully up to the wicket ... And he bowls!

*Alan 'bowls', With more energy than he intended. His towel and its contents go flying. His satchel goes with it, spilling text books and exercise books all over the pavement.*

JOHN A And Bradman yet again hooks him convulsively for four ...

*Alan kneels down and starts scrabbling his things together. Two workmen are working on a hole in the road. They stand, leaning on their spades, watching him, expressionlessly.*

  *Suddenly, Alan jerks up, in agony. He starts stamping hard up and down on one foot. He notices the two workmen still watching him, deadpan.*

ALAN It's cramp! I've got cramp! Bloody hell fire and scrotums!

*He continues stamping his foot up and down. The two workmen watch.*

WORKMAN 1 Millions of pounds on education.

WORKMAN 2 It'll be with him living under the shadow of the Bomb, I expect.

*Alan stamps his foot again, then looks down in shock and disbelief at the pavement. He's trodden on a huge spider. Out of its body run scores of very tiny spiders.*

## 4 Grammar school grounds

*Tommy, a groundsman in his mid-twenties, is marking out cricket pitches in front of the school. He looks a very worried man.*

*From inside the school building we hear schoolchildren singing the hymn at morning prayers.*

*Alan comes running into the school drive from the road, his satchel and towel once again under control. As he runs, he pulls his cap out of his pocket and stuffs it onto his head.*

*Tommy watches him, as he approaches. Looks at his watch.*

ALAN (*excitedly*) Hey, Tommy! Guess what!

TOMMY One day you'll break the school record and turn up at home-time.

ALAN I've just seen a miracle.

TOMMY I reckon you're going to bloody *need* one.

ALAN I have, honest. Just now. I was witness to a phenomenon and-or miracle!

TOMMY How many times a week do you have to be late before you get your arse hammered?

ALAN Three.

TOMMY And what's today make?

ALAN Four.

*He runs on towards the entrance of the school, then stops, turns and calls back.*

ALAN Are you feeling any happier this morning?

TOMMY Sod off in with you!

*Alan dashes off again. Tommy sighs, worriedly, and continues with his work.*

## 5 Classroom

*A co-educational class of 14-year-olds are seated at their desks, silently reading. Among them is the girl he was dreaming about earlier: Ann Lawton.*

*The teacher is Miss Land. She's in her early thirties. She's also at her desk purportedly reading. But she appears to be as worried and preoccupied as Tommy was: whatever gesture of worry (chewing his lip, pulling his ear-lobe) that he did in the previous scene, Miss Land now repeats precisely.*

*Alan tumbles into the room. Everyone immediately looks at him. And he's consequently, immediately embarrassed.*

ALAN    (*mumbling*) Sorry I'm late, Miss Land.

MISS LAND    Do you know what time school actually starts, Duckworth? (*To the rest of the class*) Anyone who says 'No, it's always started by the time he gets here' sees the Headmaster at once. (*To Alan*) You're seeing him at twelve.

ALAN    Yes, Miss, thank you, Miss.

*He makes his way to his desk. Two or three of the boys (his pals) grin at him. The others ignore him.*

MISS LAND    (*to Alan*) Silent Reading. 'The Mill on the Floss' page 380. Questions at the end of the lesson.

*Alan settles as quietly as he can (i.e. noisily) into his seat, puts books from his satchel into his desk and takes 'The Mill on the Floss' out of it. He glances at Ann. She's totally oblivious to him. He glances at one of his pals nearby. This is Abbo.*

*Abbo half-raises his arm and bends it in a sort of rickety salute, then, quietly and hoarsely moans their password.*

ABBO    P'tang, yang, kipperbang, uuuh!

ALAN    (*with the same action and sound*) P'tang, yang, kipperbang, uuuh!

MISS LAND    (*promptly*) Who was that?

*Innocent silence throughout the room. She resumes her reading and worrying. Alan turns to another pal. This is Shaz.*

ALAN    (*as before*) P'tang, yang, kipperbang, uuh!

SHAZ    P'tang, yang, kipperbang, uuh!

MISS LAND    Alright – Who's moaning and groaning!

*Again, silence and innocence reign.*

MISS LAND    The next person who moans and groans will stand outside the door while thinking of an explanation for the Headmaster.

*She – and the class – resume reading. Alan flicks through his book till he finds page 380.*

*Shaz taps him on the shoulder.*

SHAZ    (*whispering*) I wish I'd have thought of that.

ALAN    Of what?

SHAZ    'He doesn't know what time school starts, because it's always started by the time he . . .'

MISS LAND    Duckworth! Get out!

SHAZ   Please, Miss, he's only just got *in*.

MISS LAND   Both of you — outside the door. Impudence and impertinence.

*Alan and Shaz get up and make their way to the door. The others watch, trying to stifle their tittering. Alan glances at Ann. She ignores him.*

MISS LAND   Since Silent Reading appears to be a contradiction in terms, we'll now have Reading Aloud. Ann, you start. Back to page 380.

*Ann is pleased at being chosen. She smiles shyly at one of the boys in the class. This is Geoffrey. He smiles admiringly back. Ann starts to read a lyrical passage of love. Alan watches her, achingly, as he backs out of the door.*

## 6  The corridor

*Shaz and Alan stand outside the door. Through the glass door, Alan watches Ann reading, his heart melting. Miss Land catches his eye. He looks away.*

## 7  The school gym

*The boys of Alan's class, wearing vests, shorts and gym shoes, are queuing up to take their turn at the vault. One by one they thud up to a 'buck' or 'horse', and with varying degrees of success somehow get over.*

*A gym teacher stands beside the apparatus, supervising. After each vault, he calls 'Next!'*

*Alan, Abbo and Shaz are at the end of the queue, whispering to each other.*

ABBO   (*incredulously, enviously*) Inside??

SHAZ   Definitely.

ABBO   With your hand?

SHAZ   Well, what do you think? My elbow?

ABBO   She let you??

SHAZ   It was her idea!

ABBO   Actually inside her brassiere? Next to her heaving, naked, white flesh?

SHAZ   Near enough.

ABBO   (*suspiciously*) What?

SHAZ  Definitely insider her *blouse*.

*This is a terrible let-down. Abbo groans accordingly.*

SHAZ  (*hotly, defensively*) Well, it's more than *you've* ever got! (*Feebly*) Interior blouseness. (*More feebly*) Between her blouse and her brassiere. (*Even more feebly*) The real thing.

ABBO  (*disgustedly*) Sod off, Shaz!

SHAZ  For God's sake – she's not *completely* shag-nasty! I only had to give her my protractor and compass! I could hardly expect –

GYM T  (*calling*) Talking, Willoughby?

SHAZ  Er . . . no, sir. Coughing.

GYM T  You're a lying toad, Willoughby. What are you?

SHAZ  A lying toad, sir.

GYM T  Of the first what, Willoughby?

SHAZ  Of the first water, sir.

GYM T  On the wallbars, then, please. Good Friday.

SHAZ  (*protesting*) Oh, sir!

GYM T  On the count of three. Three!

*Shaz climbs up on the wallbars, then hangs from them with his arms outstretched, as though undergoing crucifixion.*

GYM T  Feet off.

*Shaz takes his feet off a supporting wallbar. He's now suspended by his hands alone. It's very painful.*

ABBO  (*whispering to Alan*) Still. Exterior brassierosity is *nearly* bare white flesh, isn't it? But for one sixteenth of an inch or something. It's better than nothing.

*A small boy (in school uniform) comes into the gym, hands the gym teacher a note, then exits.*

ALAN  Did she let him kiss her as well?

ABBO  (*disgusted again*) *Kiss* her?

ALAN  I wouldn't fancy kissing her. Osculatory weediosity.

ABBO  Kissing? He got as far as kissing her bloody weeks ago! On the fourth date!

GYM T  Duckworth! Chitty from the Headmaster. Your presence is requested in his study. Now. Go.

ALAN  (*apprehensively*) Can I just put my pants on, sir?

GYM T  Now!

ALAN  But I'll need my pants, sir! He's going to –

GYM T  Now!

*Alan exchanges grim smiles with the others and goes out. The boys continue vaulting. The gym teacher glances up at Shaz on the wallbars.*

GYM T  All right, Willoughby. Easter Monday.

*Shaz gratefully drops down from the wallbars, and ruefully rubs his biceps.*

## 8  Outside the school building

*Tommy passes by, carrying a bucket of whitewash. He glances into one of the windows, hopefully. From his point of view, we see Miss Land in her classroom, writing on the blackboard. She sees him.*

## 9  Inside the classroom

*Miss Land's face trembles on seeing Tommy. The classroom is empty apart from herself. She goes to the open window.*

TOMMY  Any news?
MISS LAND  Nothing.
TOMMY  (*heart sinking*) Nothing?
MISS LAND  Nothing.
TOMMY  (*worried sick*) Oh, hell.
MISS LAND  (*bitterly*) Exactly. A *living* hell, thank you!

*She slams the window shut.*

## 10  The Headmaster's study

*The Headmaster is taking some notes out of his briefcase as Alan arrives. The Headmaster is in his sixties; exhausted, but drily amused, by the disappointments of life and career.*
*There's a knock at the door.*

HEAD  Come!

*The door opens and Alan enters, still wearing his vest and shorts. He closes the door and stands waiting. The Headmaster goes to the desk to scrutinize an attendance register.*

HEAD  Duckworth, is it?
ALAN  Yes, sir, thank you, sir.

HEAD  (*checking in the register*) Persistently late, four times.

ALAN  Yes, sir.

HEAD  (*checking again*) Weren't you given detention for the first two?

ALAN  Yes, sir.

HEAD  (*checking again*) And were late for that as well . . .

ALAN  Just slightly, sir.

*The Headmaster sighs, gets a cane from his collection and flexes it in front of Alan.*

HEAD  As you well know, Duckworth, I don't believe in corporal punishment.

ALAN  No, sir.

HEAD  I'd therefore prefer you to regard what's about to happen purely as a deterrent.

ALAN  Yes, sir, thank you, sir.

HEAD  Bend over.

ALAN  The reason today, sir, was I saw a miracle. A scientific miracle. I was –

HEAD  A lifetime in the teaching profession, laddie, has taught me that miracles are for weekends and holidays only. Toes, please.

*He flexes the cane. Alan bends over. As the Headmaster raises the cane, we hear –*

JOHN A  And it's Keith Miller now, bat menacingly poised facing Jim Laker.

*The cane swishes down.*

JOHN A  And, with a flick of the wrist, Miller drives him savagely through the covers for four . . .

*The cane thwacks against Alan's backside. He jerks up; then he and the Headmaster prepare for the second stroke.*

JOHN A  And Laker refashions his grip on the ball, turns, and strides, and he bowls . . .

*The cane comes swishing down again.*

JOHN A  . . . and Miller dances down the wicket and slashes him viciously to the boundary.

*The cane cracks down again on Alan's backside. He jerks in pain.*

JOHN A  And that's the end of the over.

*Alan stands up.*

HEAD  One more for luck, Duckworth.

JOHN A  Sorry, I miscounted. Wishful thinking on my part and no doubt, England's. There's one more to come. And Jim Laker peers at the scoreboard, peers at . . .

*Alan bends down again. The Headmaster prepares for the third stroke.*

JOHN A  . . . Miller, and, I fancy, peers deep into his own soul, trundles back and bowls –

*The cane cracks down for the third time.*

JOHN A  And it's a six! Laker rolls his eyes up to the St John's Wood heaven in search, but little hope, of justice.

*Alan straightens up, red-faced and in agony.*

HEAD  Off you pop, laddie. No rubbing better till you're back in class. And, even then, only within reason in front of female members of staff.

*Alan walks stiffly out.*

### 11  The school dining room

*The first sitting is in progress, supervised by two or three teachers. A babble of conversation among the children as they eat – kept just below the level of the sound of the cutlery. Alan is at a table with the other boys from his class. The girls are at a table of their own. Alan is half-standing.*

BOY 1  How many did you get? Corporal or Sergeant?

ALAN  Sergeant.

*Alan is farming out his meal onto his pals' plates. They accept this as normal.*

BOY 2  Can I have your pudding?

ALAN  It's Abbo's turn for my pudding.

BOY 2  Don't you ever die of mass starvation?

*Alan looks across at Ann at her table; animated conversation around her. She looks up from her plate, looks across in Alan's direction, and then – to Alan's excited, incredulous disbelief – she coyly smiles.*

*He half-smiles back, then with sudden suspicion, glances over his shoulder to see if it's someone else she's actually smiling at. His suspicions are correct.*

*She's smiling at Geoffrey. He smiles back at her. She blushes and gets on with her dinner. Alan stays in his half-standing position, not quite knowing what to do with the half-smile still frozen on his face.*

*He points it in different directions aimlessly, then, while pretending to listen to the conversation around him, with exaggerated interest, he lets it fade away.*

### 12 The boys' lavatories (a little later)

*Some graffiti on the cubicle doors is limited to the mildness of 'Kilroy was here', 'B.T. = J.S. true' and drawings of 'Charlie' peering over brick walls, above slogans like 'Wot, no knickers?'*

*Abbo, Shaz and Alan are seated on the floor, playing pontoon. (Again, Alan is only half-seated).*

ABBO  Twist.

*Alan hands him the nine of spades.*

ALAN  Nine.
ABBO  Bust.

*He throws his cards in.*

ALAN  Shaz?
SHAZ  I said I'm sticking.

*Alan shows his cards. Two tens.*

ALAN  Pay twenty-ones.
SHAZ  *(revealing King and Ace)* Pay me.
ABBO  Jammy sod.

*Alan hands the pack to Shaz, who starts shuffling the cards.*

ALAN  Have you ever trodden on a big fat spider and seen millions of little spiders come running out?
SHAZ  *(handing cards to Abbo)* Cut.
ALAN  Well, have you?
SHAZ  *(taking cut pack back and starting dealing)* Have we what?
ALAN  God, deafness incorporated! Have you ever burst a great bulbous spider – and thousands of miniature ones come dashing out?

SHAZ No.

ALAN What would you think if you did? Twist.

SHAZ (*dealing card*) Queen.

ABBO That I'd been overdoing it and my mind had gone for a burton.

SHAZ Are you sticking?

ALAN (*slightly disturbed*) Overdoing what?

*The others look at him, deadpan.*

ABBO Well, *what*?

ALAN (*self-consciously*) Oh. (*Pause*) Um . . . no, twist.

SHAZ (*dealing card*) Nine.

ALAN Overdoing it with a girl, you mean?

*Shaz and Abbo look at him, witheringly.*

ABBO Not with a girl! If you had a girl you'd have no need to do it at all, would you?

ALAN (*guiltily*) Oh, that. (*Pause*) Overdoing it can't make you think you've seen spiders, can it? Twist.

ABBO (*bewildered*) How can he twist! He's already got –

SHAZ Why? *Have* you been? (*Deals card*) King.

ALAN What – seeing them or overdoing it?

*Abbo grabs Alan's cards and turns them over, incredulously.*

ABBO 48! He's bust 27 times over!

ALAN I haven't been doing *either*.

ABBO Sod off, Quack-Quack. You're getting on my nerves! (*Turns his cards over*) Pontoon.

SHAZ Match null and void. Ungentlemanly play from Quack-Quack.

ABBO I had bloody pontoon!

SHAZ (*to Alan*) Go on! Scarper! (*Calls to cubicles*) Anyone in there fancy some pontoonicosity?

VOICE What are you playing for?

SHAZ Sweet coupons.

VOICE Hang on a sec.

*Alan wanders out. A troubled pause.*

ABBO I *never* get pontoon . . .

SHAZ There was a boy in this Hollywood Snack Bar who knew a bloke whose cousin did it with a Butlin's redcoat in her chalet.

ABBO (*deeply impressed*) What – the lot?
SHAZ The whole hog. Completely bare.

*A pause. They both mull over the thought, miserably, riven with envy.*

VOICE Did he say what it was like?
SHAZ He's booked again for *next* year . . .

## 13 The classroom (a little later)

*The girls of Alan's class are informally gathered around one of the desks, seated, kneeling, lolling about. Ann is with them. Standing on the seat of the desk is one of the girls, Eunice. She holds a sheet of paper and a pencil.*

EUNICE Next is Shaz. How many for Shaz?

*Two of the girls raise their hands. The others giggle at them. Eunice write '2' against Shaz's name.*

EUNICE Next – Laurence. How many?

*One girl puts her hand up. The others giggle.*

GIRL 1 He's not all that bad . . .
GIRL 2 He's grotesque to the nth degree!
GIRL 1 His *quiff's* nice.

*The others whoop at her. Eunice records a '1' against his name.*

EUNICE Next is . . . (*her voice betrays here own excitement*) Geoffrey. Geoffrey Whittaker?

*All the girls raise their hands. Some of them turn to Ann and giggle enviously. Ann looks modestly delighted.*

## 14 The school grounds (a little later)

*A few children are dotted around, talking together, or throwing tennis balls or playing a scratch game of rounders.*
*Tommy – looking even more worried than before – is marking out a cricket pitch. Alan is strolling along beside him, talking with great self-assurance and enthusiasm. As he walks along, he occasionally goes through the motion of bowling a cricket ball or playing a batting stroke.*

ALAN   . . . which means that, from now on, there'll never be any
more wars. Ever again. For the simple raison d'être that
the United Nations will *insist* there's no more wars! Any
country wants to invade another – well, hard cheddar, oppo!
– the United Nations'll vote against it. Q.E.D.

*Tommy is too preoccupied with his own problems to even listen. He
just grunts vague agreement. Alan warms to his theme.*

ALAN   So, what you and all the other Tommies did . . . What you
all did, with our gallant allies and comrades across the seas
and Commonwealth and that, facing the foe in whatever
theatre of human conflict . . . (*Trying to remember previous
conversations*) at . . . um . . . where was it . . . ?

TOMMY   (*still not listening*) Dunkirk, El Alamein, the Battle of the
Bulge and Burma.

ALAN   Dunkirk, El Alamein, the Battle of the Bulge and
Burma . . . what you did was not just defeat Hitler's
Germany and Japan's . . . Japan. I mean, let's face it. You
changed the future of the world!

*Alan has been crowding slightly into Tommy while enthusing.*

TOMMY   You're in my way a bit.

*Alan realises; moves to one side a little.*

ALAN   Sorry. Apologydom commensurate. (*Glances at Tommy.
Finally becomes aware of his mood*) Is it still worrying you?

TOMMY   What?

ALAN   I don't know . . . Whatever's been worrying you.

TOMMY   I'll survive.

ALAN   Is it the Australians winning the test?

TOMMY   Mmm? No, no. It's nothing. Nothing to worry about.

*A boy and girl (a little older than Alan) emerge from the back of the
cricket pavilion. They cross the cricket pitch, looking a little
dishevelled, embarrassed and guilty. The boy grins shamefacedly at
Alan.*

BOY 3   (*half-raising his arm*) P'tang, yang, kipperbang, uuh!

ALAN   (*reflexively; a little bemused*) P'tang, yang, kipperbang, uuh!

*The boy and girl part. She goes towards other girls who are playing;
the boy goes towards other boys. Alan watches them go . . . He's once
again beginning to feel on the brink of tears. A pause.*

ALAN   Pound to a penny, he's been trying to kiss her.

*Tommy looks at him, incredulously.*

TOMMY   'Kiss' her?

ALAN   Pound to a penny.

*Tommy sits down and starts rolling a cigarette. Alan still stands watching the boy and girl.*

TOMMY   Have *you* got a girl-friend?

ALAN   I've got red hands.

TOMMY   (*blankly*) Eh?

*The words begin to tumble out, with a sad matter-of-factness, devoid of self-pity.*

ALAN   The skin's very red and thin, like transparent, with chewed-up nails ... I hate my hands. And my neck – that's thin as well. And my feet sweat. *And* my hands. That's probably why they're always red. My face goes red a lot as well. Not blushing, I don't think. I don't blush. I just sometimes go red. It's only a phase. Bums are nothing really. Everyone's got a bum. Always have had. They're nothing to be ashamed of. Dicks aren't either. Everyone's got a dick. It's only the human torso. Tits included. They're just for feeding babies with, deep down. Not for bouncing about. The same goes for getting a feel and dry rubs when you're snogging. Kissing's different. A kiss is ...

*He peters into silence, now fighting back hot tears. A pause. Tommy is smiling at him, sadly.*

TOMMY   (*gently*) Girls like it as well, you know.

ALAN   Like what?

TOMMY   What boys like. (*Then with a touch of bitterness*) Some of them bloody *love* it.

*A pause.*

ALAN   I'm not talking about just French girls.

TOMMY   (*baffled*) *I'm* not.

ALAN   Anyway, I don't bother, myself. I've got my cricket. Best get back.

*He starts off back to the school building. Tommy sighs deeply; draws on his rolled cigarette.*

17

## 15 The classroom (a little later)

*Alan enters. Eunice and the other girls are roughly as we last saw them, but now giggling secretively among themselves. The boys are lounging around their (own) desks. Eunice climbs onto her seat, as Alan comes in, and claps her hands for attention.*

EUNICE Attention, please, males of the species! (*The noise lessens a little*) May I have bags of hush, please! (*She gets it*) Thank you. We, the girls of 4B, have voted on who is the dishiest boy in the class.

*Abbo cranes his head downwards and to one side, to look – unsuccessfully – up her legs.*

ABBO Green ones in the wash, Eunice?

EUNICE Shut your face, pig-features!

ABBO (*to Shaz*) 'Pig-features'. I assume I didn't get her vote, then.

EUNICE Look, belt up, everybody, it's nearly half-past. (*They quieten down again*) The votes for each boy are as follows, viz: 'Dishiest-boy-in-the-class-contest': first, Geoffrey, eight votes.

*Geoffrey shrugs off the catcalls of the other boys, good-naturedly and a little embarrassedly – then exchanges a smile with Ann.*

EUNICE Second, Phillip, four votes. (*More catcalls. Alan waits tensely for the next name*) Third equals – Clogger, Robert, Creeping Syrup and Steven – three votes. (*More reactions. Alan's heart is sinking*) Fourth, Shaz, two votes. (*Shaz joins his hands above his head like a champion. Abbo jeers. Alan swallows*) Fifth equals – Quasimodo, Laurence, Peter, Four-Eyes and Pot – one vote. And last – and definitely least – (*All the girls are now in fits of giggles. Alan wants to die*) Abbo – no votes!

*The girls laugh and applaud. The boys rag Abbo.*

SHAZ Give him the money, Barney!

*Alan stands watching them all, numbly. Abruptly the bell rings for the beginning of lessons. The hubbub immediately dies down and everyone scrambles to their seats, opening their desks to take out French grammars and textbooks.*

*In the scramble, Eunice's list of votes flutters to the floor between the children's desks and the teacher's.*

*Alan is still standing where he was.*

ALAN   *(almost inaudibly)* How many did *I* get? *(To nearest girl, as he starts for his desk)* Majorie, how many did *I* get?

MARJORIE   What?

ALAN   No, I was just remarking.

*Marjorie stares at him for a moment.*

MARJORIE   Oh, blood and sand!

*She turns to Eunice, as the French teacher, a middle-aged man, enters and goes to his desk. Everyone faces front, looking academically expectant.*

MARJORIE   *(whispering)* Eunice, we forgot to vote for Quack-Quack!

EUNICE   Mmm? *(looks at Alan, realises)* Oh, sorry, Quack-Quack. We didn't have you down …

FRENCH T   'Monsieur et Madame Desgranges', book four. 'Les Vacances de Monsieur et Madame Desgranges au Bord de la Mer.'

*Alan can hardly see the page in his book through his tears. He looks across at Ann, then at Geoffrey. Both are immersed in their books.*
    *During the following speech, the French teacher notices the voting list on the floor, leaves his desk, picks it up, glances at it in mild puzzlement, then stuffs it in his pocket and returns to his desk.*

JOHN A   Well, cricket can be a cruel game. It seems now that England are faced with an impossible task. 364 behind and playing like a bunch of schoolgirls. It's enough to make strong men weep. However, it's a funny old game this cricket. It's been said before and, no doubt, will again …

### 16 The Headmaster's study (mid-afternoon)

*The Headmaster is seated at his desk. Seated opposite him is Miss Land.*

JOHN A   … that a game is never lost till it's won. We shall see.

MISS LAND   *(worriedly)* I'm sorry, sir. I can't do drama. Not this term.

HEAD   The school play is hardly drama, Estelle. Three evenings rehearsal a week for three weeks … I've had it all marked up on graph paper with the dates in red and everything …

MISS LAND   I'm sorry, sir … I'm … well, I've things on my mind, just at the present … And please don't call me Estelle.

HEAD   *(smiles)* Aren't we forgetting something, Estelle?

MISS LAND (*warily*) Are we?

HEAD You can't learn to play the game of rugby till you've learnt to play the game of life.

MISS LAND (*pause, then blankly*) I'm not taking rugby as *well*, am I?

HEAD (*a pause, then equally blankly*) It's a saying.

MISS LAND Ah.

*The Headmaster picks up one of the four identical slim books from the desk.*

HEAD 'The Tables Turned', a play in one act, suitable for schools, by P. J. Latimer, M. A. Oxon. A cast of two boys, one girl, and we can use the same scenery from last year's triumph.

MISS LAND (*firmly*) It's just that these next few weeks until the end of term are a bit ... I'd be grateful, sir, if someone else could ...

HEAD (*smiles, a little sadly*) Seems silly calling me sir, when there's no one else in the room.

MISS LAND Please.

HEAD (*puts his hand on hers*) I never see you these days, Estelle ...

MISS LAND (*pulls her hand away*) Those days are over, sir. These days aren't those days. The war's been over a long time now.

HEAD And all the *young* men have come marching home again, eh?

MISS LAND (*troubled*) I thought we agreed to draw a veil over the war, Henry. Ever since V. J. night.

*A silence. Both remember their past.*

HEAD Ah, well ... One man's war, another man's ...

*Another silence. He remembers their passion sadly, tenderly. She squirms a little uncomfortably.*

HEAD Those days you kept me young. These days all I do is get older. Sometimes in morning assembly, I fall asleep during 'Onward Christian Soldiers'.

MISS LAND (*a small smile*) Who doesn't?

HEAD While I'm actually *singing* it, though.

*Miss Land sighs, defeated, and picks up the four copies of the play.*

MISS LAND Well, I can't guarantee it'll be Mrs Miniver ...

HEAD Thank you, Estelle.

MISS LAND You're welcome, sir.

## 17 The school grounds

*The kids are leaving at the end of the day. Apart from two or three surreptitious couples, boys are mostly with boys, and girls with girls.*

## 18 The classroom

*A couple of girls are stuffing homework into their satchels and making for the door. They completely ignore the daily end-of-day routine which is being carried out across the room by the windows.*

*The routine is this: Eunice stands with her back to the wall, blowing bubble-gum, as the boys, their homework in their satchels, form a queue in front of her. Each boy, in turn, then presses his body against Eunice's for a moment with complete absence of passion, then wanders from the room to go home.*

*As each boy presses against her, Eunice – automatically and unconvincingly – complains: 'Honestly, you're terrible/ You boys, really!/ A girl just isn't safe! /You're horrible ... it's every night, the same/ I'm disgusted with you, I am truly ...'*

*Alan is now at the head of the queue. He presses himself against her. In mid-press, he glances through the window.*

*From his point of view, we see Ann and Geoffrey talking shyly together on the way home.*

*Eunice immediately becomes aware of a stirring in Alan's loins – and naturally, if wrongly, assumes she's the cause.*

EUNICE Hey! You can quit that for a kick-off! Crude pig!

ALAN *(preoccupied, watching Ann)* Mmm?

EUNICE You've had your ration, Quack-Quack. Sod off!

ALAN *(glances down, realises what's happening)* Oh. Sorry, Eunice.

*He turns and joins Abbo at the door. Shaz has his press with Eunice, then goes over to Alan and Abbo and exits with them.*

## 19 A street outside school grounds

*Groups of kids are on their way home. Talking, playing, fighting and teasing. Boys and girls are separate, except for Ann and Geoffrey who are walking along together, sharing a little laugh now and then, almost touching hands.*

*Some way behind are Abbo, Shaz and Alan throwing, kicking or heading a tennis ball as they go. Alan is trying to keep his eye on Ann – and consequently keeps missing the ball.*

*As they round the corner, out of sight from the school, the boys take their caps off and stuff them in their pockets; the girls do the same with their school hats and ties.*

## 20 The school grounds

*Tommy is wearily trudging from the playing fields towards the school building, lugging bits of groundsman's equipment with him.*

*Miss Land emerges from the school entrance, riding her bicycle, starting for home. Tommy catches up with her.*

*Both look as depressed as ever. Tommy looks at her, enquiringly. She shakes her head bitterly. His face falls.*

| | |
|---|---|
| TOMMY | Still? |
| MISS LAND | (*uneasily*) We can be seen! |
| TOMMY | Still nothing? |
| MISS LAND | Oh, for God's sake! |
| TOMMY | Is there anything I can do? |
| MISS LAND | I think you've done enough already, don't you? |

*She rides off. He watches, his stomach churning.*

## 21 A street corner (some time later)

*Ann and Geoffrey have stopped at the corner. They stand chatting to each other for a moment – then wave cheerio and go off in different directions.*

*Alan, Shaz and Abbo wander into view; Alan still keeping a beady eye on Ann.*

ALAN   ... because what he did, in Dunkirk, El Alamein, the Battle of the Bulge and Burma, was change the future of mankind. On those far-off shores and foreign climes, with his courage and heroism above and beyond the call of –

*They've reached the corner. Alan starts off – with attempted nonchalance – in the same direction as Ann.*

| | |
|---|---|
| ALAN | Anyway, see you tomorrow, modern generation. |
| ABBO | (*puzzled*) Where are you going? |
| ALAN | Errand for my dad. Paternal jobosity. |
| SHAZ | Where? |
| ALAN | (*indicating vaguely*) Palmerston Avenue way ... |
| ABBO | Well, don't walk too fast. You'll catch Smelly Lawton up. |

ALAN   (*innocuously*) Smelly Lawton?

*Abbo nods, towards Ann walking down the street. Alan follows his glance – and feigns surprise on seeing her.*

ALAN   (*grins*) Hell, I've better things to do with *my* shoe leather than catch *her* up! See you tomorrow, men.

SHAZ   Coming to the flicks tonight?

ALAN   (*pats his satchel*) Homework. I've got double Cicero for hand-farting in Latin. (*He presses the back of his hand against his mouth and makes rasping noises in demonstration.*) P'tang, yang, kipperbang, uuh!

SHAZ   P'tang, yang, kipperbang, uuh!

ABBO   P'tang, yang, kipperbang, uuh!

*Shaz and Abbo wander off in one direction. Alan nonchalantly follows Ann.*

## 22  Palmerston Avenue (a few minutes later)

*His heart thumping, Alan is still trailing Ann; keeping a safe distance behind her ... but getting nearer ... and nearer ... and nearer ... During this, we hear –*

JOHN A   And so, with 365 runs still to get and now only one wicket remaining before inevitable and overwhelming defeat, in comes the last England batsman ... (*He gasps*) And, I don't believe it! It's unbelievable. All of Lords is flabbergasted. Making his way to the wicket, and in doing so making his test debut, is a schoolboy. It's unheard of. Who could he be? Well, his name, apparently is Alan Duckworth. He's fourteen years old and he's known to his friends as Quack-Quack. Can this callow youth save the day for England? Can this fourteen-year-old cricketer make a schoolboy dream come true? Can this young warrior – striding out, stiffening his slender neck – can he change the course of Destiny? Well, now's his big chance.

*Ann turns into the gateway of her house. At the front door, she glances – with no interest whatever – in Alan's direction. He immediately drops on one knee to tie a shoelace that doesn't need tying. She goes into her house. The door closes behind her.*

JOHN A   And Duckworth's courage fails him. And Lindwall knows it.

23

*Alan walks past Ann's house, looking straight ahead. As soon as he's passed it, he swivels right round on his heel and walks back the way he came.*

*His eyes prick with frustration and unrequited passion and self-anger.*

JOHN A   And Duckworth, bat between his legs, looks as though he's trying to pretend he's not even there. He's a bit of a lolloper, this boy. He lollops. And he turns back towards the pavilion. Has he given up already? Or is he going to change his bat? In either event, he appears just a little annoyed with himself, just a little frustrated.

## 23   Outside Alan's house (ten minutes later)

*Still on the brink of tears, Alan walks towards the house. As he walks, he kicks stones violently, swings his satchel at walls and then swings it at his own head.*

*The two workmen are watching him, deadpan.*

*Alan kicks at a half-brick on the pavement and nearly breaks his toes. When he reaches his front door, he bangs his head violently on it three or four times, then puts his key in the lock and opens it.*

ALAN   (*brave face; calling inside*) I've arrived, and to prove it I'm here.

*He goes in.*

*The two workmen stand looking at the closed door for a long moment. Then –*

WORKMAN 1   I blame Dicky Valentine and Lita Rosa.

## 24   Alan's bedroom (night)

*Alan is in bed; his right hand under the bedclothes, his left hand on top.*

ALAN   I followed her down her street for You. I thought that might have given you a good opportunity. But it was not to be. So please, God, let it be tomorrow, if poss. Or the day after. Or, at the latest, before the end of term. I'll never last the summer holidays without kissing her. Kissing her. Kissing her. On her lips. Ann's lips. Kissing her lips. Kissing her lips. Kissing her. Please help me. If you could just see your way to taking some of the red out of my hands and thicken

24

my neck out and stop my feet ponging and let me kiss Ann's lips. And, please, let Tommy cheer up and not be so depressed and let England beat Australia and let the spider that I split in two be all right, and please God, let me stop crying all the time. (*Now almost in tears*) I wouldn't if You'd just let me kiss her. I'd never cry again. (*He takes his right hand out from under the bedclothes. It's wearing a boxing glove. He half-raises it to God*) P'tang, yang, kipperbang, uuh!

## 25  The school cricket pavilion (night)

*The school is in darkness. A faint light glows from the pavilion.*

MISS LAND  Well, *say* something!
TOMMY  There's nothing left to say, is there?

## 26  Inside the cricket pavilion

*Miss Land and Tommy are seated, despondently, among the sports- and ground-maintenance equipment. An atmosphere of leaden gloom.*

MISS LAND  No.
TOMMY  I mean, fair's fair, marriage is out of the question, isn't it?
MISS LAND  (*bitterly*) Thank you! So much for the Age of Chivalry!
TOMMY  I mean you'd get the sack!
MISS LAND  I know what you mean, thank you! (*Pause: then emptily*) I don't even *like* you.
TOMMY  I know. (*Flatly*) *You* give *me* the screaming ab-dabs.
MIS LAND  We're just not each other's type.
TOMMY  No.

*A helpless silence.*

TOMMY  Up the creek without a paddle.

*Miss Land quietly starts to cry.*

TOMMY  Maybe it's just the weather . . . sometimes the weather makes women . . . or the *worry* . . .
MISS LAND  How can it be the worry?! I wouldn't *have* the worry if it wasn't for the worry.
TOMMY  Has it never been like this before?
MISS LAND  You *know* it hasn't!
TOMMY  I mean . . . before me.
MISS LAND  (*staring at him, appalled and insulted*) What are you suggesting?

TOMMY Well, fair's fair, I wasn't the first, was I?

MISS LAND Virtually.

TOMMY You *know* I wasn't.

MISS LAND Apart from ... in the war. With a respectable, married man. Not young. A ... a professional man ... academically. He was the only one before you. (*Pause*) Apart from a few times just after the war with the American Quarter-Master Sergeant.

TOMMY (*shocked*) Americans!

MISS LAND (*guiltily*) *One*! *One* American! (*Pause*) Virtually.

TOMMY Old men and Yanks! Bloody old two-faced fogeys and randy Yanks! While me and my oppos are spilling blood and guts all over Africa and France and the sodding Rhineland!

*A pause. A stillness.*

MISS LAND (*quietly*) It seemed a good idea at the time. I thought it might lead to ... something. I couldn't read the future, could I? I didn't know one day I was going to be stuck with *you*.

*Another pause. Tommy wrestles with his thoughts.*

TOMMY And were you ... was it ever this late with *them*?

MISS LAND It can't have been, can it, Tommy? Otherwise I *definitely* wouldn't be stuck here with you ...!


## 27 The staff common room

*Three or four teachers scattered about, having cups of tea, reading, marking exercise books, snoozing.*

   *Miss Land is reading her copy of 'The Tables Turned', grim-faced.*

   *The French Teacher pulls his pipe from his pocket. With it comes Eunice's crumpled voting list. He straightens it out again, glances at it, shakes his head, then looks across at Miss Land.*

FRENCH T Estelle, were you aware that Geoffrey Whittaker is the matinee idol of 4B?

MISS LAND Sorry?

FRENCH T (*glances again at the list*) I assume that 'dishiest' means the only one sans pimples.

*He hands her the list. Miss Land looks at it, thoughtfully.*

### 28  The cricket pavilion (dinnertime)

*Tommy is despondently nibbling at sandwiches from an army satchel. Alan is perched on the seat of the lawn-mower.*

ALAN  (*enthusiastically*) . . . because, by ensuring victory over the Axis Powers and Huns, what you've done is a) ensure peace for all mankind full stop, b) make all men brothers for ever, irrespective of race, colour or whatisit – doofer – creed, and c) ended the class struggle – so that, from now on, there'll never again be poverty, disease and hunger – and everyone will be equal, with a full and rich life, probably all speaking Esperanto. The best example is teasmaids.

TOMMY  (*staring at him*) What?

ALAN  Teasmaids.

TOMMY  What about them?

ALAN  For a cup of tea when you wake up.

TOMMY  They're the best example of what?

ALAN  Of what I've been saying. In time, everyone on earth'll have a teasmaid, irrespective of race, colour or creed. You can't stop progress. (*Satisfied smile*) I bet that's something you never thought of at El Alamein.

*Tommy sighs, stuffs his sandwiches back in the satchel.*

TOMMY  Can't eat. Won't go down. As bad as you.

ALAN  (*looks at watch*) Hell's bells! I'm late!

TOMMY  (*jerking a guilty look at him*) Who? (*Alan starts running off towards the school building.*) Oh . . . for *lessons* . . .

### 29  Fields near the school

*Alan's class, led by a female botany teacher, are in the middle of a Nature Study lesson, beneath a beech tree. They're all examining the leaves of the tree, and drawing copies of them in their exercise books.*

*Alan is staring at Ann, in a world of his own. In – and from – his point of view, she looks like a Pre-Raphaelite beauty. Her face and hair are bathed in shimmering, golden sunlight filtering through the trees.*

BOTANY T  (*holding a growing leaf*) . . . which, unlike the oak leaf, is ovate-elliptic rather than triangular, although acute at the apex . . . Notice the straight lateral nerves are slightly-toothed. They appear in early May as the tree

27

begins to flower ... And here it's similar to the oak in that the flowers are unisexual, the females in clusters on their stalks, the males globular and pendulous ... Duckworth!

*He's too spellbound to hear.*

BOTANY T Duckworth!

*He turns.*

BOTANY T Well?

ALAN I didn't hear the question, Miss.

BOTANY I didn't ask you one.

ALAN Oh.

ABBO (*whispering to Shaz*) Which accounts for him not hearing one. Logicosity incarcerate.

BOTANY T (*to Alan*) You're daydreaming again. The whole point of Nature Study is to study nature.

ALAN Yes, Miss.

BOTANY T And daydreaming isn't studying Nature, is it?

*On the contrary, since Ann is both the subject of his day-dreaming and the Nature specimen being studied, Alan thinks it is.*

BOTANY T Is it?

ALAN No ... no, Miss.

### 30 The classroom

*Now almost beside herself with worry, Miss Land is taking the class in English.*

MISS LAND Which, while not a simile, of course, nor in the strict sense even a metaphor, is nevertheless an example of George Eliot's consistent use of ...

*She loses concentration and peters into silence. A pause. One by one, the kids look up from their books, puzzled. She continues to stare blankly into space. One or two of the kids nudge each other. Others begin to titter. She suddenly resurfaces with a jolt. Realises what's happened.*

MISS LAND Um ... as I was saying ... (*Troubled pause*) Um ... what *was* I saying?

GEOFFREY About it not being a metaphor, Miss.

MISS LAND Exactly, Whittaker. (*Dubious pause*) Um ... about *what* not being a metaphor?

GEOFFREY  George Eliot's imagery, Miss.

MISS LAND  Well done, Whittaker. Thank goodness *someone* in class is paying attention. Come here a moment.

*He goes to her. She hands him a copy of 'The Tables Turned'.*

MISS LAND  I'm very pleased with you, Whittaker. Instead of giving you a star, I'm going to *make* you one . . .

GEOFFREY  Beg pardon, Miss?


### 31  Countryside (industrial)

*In the distance, we see a lone figure running towards us, in football shirt, shorts, socks and gym shoes. It's Geoffrey leading the field on a cross-country run. Way behind him is another boy. Further behind, a clutch of two or three boys. Straggling far behind are the rest of the runners.*

*Far, far behind the last of these, come Alan, Abbo and Shaz. Whereas everyone else is bursting his lungs, they're just strolling along.*

ALAN  Esperanto and teasmaids apart, I'll tell you something else – the future industry of the future will be university scarves . . .

ABBO  (*to Shaz*) Where was she standing?

SHAZ  Outside the British Home Stores.

ALAN  For the simple raison d'être that, from now on, everyone in the world'll go to university . . .

ABBO  How do you know she was one of them?

SHAZ  You could tell.

ABBO  Was she blonde with a slit up the side of her skirt?

SHAZ  They don't all have slits up their skirts!

ALAN  You see, now that we've won the war –

ABBO  Well, they don't carry a placard saying 'Hello, dearies, short time – seven-and-six'!

SHAZ  No one said they did.

ALAN  – we now have to win the peace . . . the whatisit . . . the aftermath.

ABBO  Well, how could you tell then!

SHAZ  She had a chain round her ankle.

ALAN  (*astounded*) The clippie on the school bus wears a chain round her ankle!

SHAZ  Well, *she's* one then.

ALAN  She's not – she's a bloody clippie!

SHAZ During the day, yes. She probably just does part-time. In the evenings. Some of them just do part-time. The nymphomaniacs.

*They walk on, each preoccupied – and a little troubled – by the subject.*

ABBO Is that what they charge? Seven-and-six?

ALAN It was you that said seven-and-six.

ABBO I know, but I'm not all that –

SHAZ Some do. Some charge eight bob. The blondes.

ABBO For the lot?

SHAZ The whole hog. Everying. Completely bare. (*Pause*) They won't *kiss*, though. That's an unwritten rule.

ALAN (*stops dead*) They won't *kiss*?

SHAZ Unheard of.

ALAN Why?

SHAZ Never do. They only kiss their ponces. They won't kiss ordinary fellers.

ABBO Even when they're . . . you know . . . doing it?

SHAZ It's their way of stating it's not true love or anything.

ALAN (*suddenly, passionately*) That's my whole point!!

*The others stare at him, puzzled. A pause.*

ABBO *What* point?

ALAN (*backtracking, defensively*) No . . . I mean . . . it's understandable . . .

SHAZ It's bloody crackers. Who wants to kiss them anyway?

ABBO Better things to do than kiss them!

SHAZ Definitely.

*They have now reached a crossroads. Now running towards them is Geoffrey, still leading the field, and nearing collapse. Abbo, Shaz and Alan step out from their short-cut and look at him indulgently, as he nears them.*

ABBO (*in deep voice*) And the next object is . . . a silly, twisted Neddy Seagoon.

SHAZ (*in deep voice*) . . . A silly, twisted Neddy Seagoon.

ALAN ('*posh*' *female voice*) Is it animal, vegetable or mineral – or Geoffrey?

*He throws them a dirty look, they fall in behind him and trot along in second place.*

ABBO   Anyway, *Grandmas* are for kissing.

SHAZ   Kissing's like shaking hands.

ALAN   No one said it wasn't.

## 32  The corridor

*It's empty. Suddenly the school bell begins to clang the end of the day. Almost at once, kids start to tumble noisily from the classrooms, carrying their satchels.*

*Ann and Geoffrey emerge from their classroom, followed by the girls of 4B (with the exception of Eunice). Miss Land, as depressed as usual, is fighting her way down the corridor through the mob. Suddenly she stops – and watches Ann and Geoffrey with interest for a moment, then calls to Ann.*

*Ann turns, separates from Geoffrey, guiltily. Miss Land goes over to her and speaks to her while handing her a copy of 'The Tables Turned'. Ann jumps up and down in excitement. Geoffrey is delighted.*

*Miss Land then continues shouldering her way through the mob towards her classroom.*

*She opens the door – and goes in.*

## 33  The classroom

*Miss Land enters. She stops rooted in her tracks at what meets her eyes – which is Eunice being 'pressed' by Alan, taking his turn in the queue of boys for the end-of-day routine.*

MISS LAND   *(aghast)* Duckworth!!

*Everyone turns and freezes.*

MISS LAND   What the hell are you doing?

ALAN   Um . . . nothing, Miss.

MISS LAND   All of you – out!

EUNICE   *(innocently)* Please, Miss, I was just getting my homework, and suddenly, out of the blue, they all –

MISS LAND   Out! All of you! Filth! Beasts of the Fields! Get out!

*They all start scrambling for the door.*

MISS LAND   *(to Alan)* Not you, Beast of the Field.

*Alan stands, stomach churning, while the room clears. Miss Land goes slowly to her desk and sits down.*

MISS LAND　Come here.

*He goes to her desk and stands there. She fixes him with hostile, disgusted eyes for a long moment. He swallows. The look continues. He glances away. Then at his shoes. Then back at Miss Land. The look continues. Then finally –*

MISS LAND　I'm not pleased with you, Duckworth.

ALAN　No, Miss.

MISS LAND　You're never here when school starts. When you *are* here, you're in a trance. When you're not in a trance, you're moaning and groaning. When you're not moaning and groaning, you're behaving like a beast of the field. You're a weed and a mess and a lolloper. You lollop.

ALAN　Yes, Miss.

MISS LAND　Is that what we fought a war for?

ALAN　No, Miss.

MISS LAND　Well, it's time you pulled your socks up.

ALAN　Yes, Miss.

MISS LAND　I'm therefore selecting you to be in the school play (*hands him a copy of 'The Tables Turned'*) Your part is Antoine, the philanderer.

ALAN　(*utterly bemused*) Pardon?

MISS LAND　Your mouth's open. Close it. (*He does so*) Rehearsal every Monday, Wednesday and Friday after school . . .

ALAN　Miss! I can't act, Miss!!

MISS LAND　Four till five in the main hall.

ALAN　Miss! I can't *act*!

MISS LAND　Acting is pretending, Duckworth. I'm sure you pretend to be a human being at home, don't you? Instead of just a lolloper?

ALAN　Miss! Honest to God, I can't stand up in front of –

MISS LAND　Your fellow thespians are Whittaker and Ann Lawton.

*Her attention is suddenly diverted by the appearance of Tommy's worried face at the window. He looks at her questioningly – already beginning to shake his head, apprehensively, at the expected reply. She grimly shakes hers, confirming the answer to his question. He sighs, and goes on his way. She sighs deeply, then returns her attention to Alan.*

*He's staring at her, open-mouthed, his heart thudding.*

ALAN　Ann Lawton?

MISS LAND　What?

ALAN   With Ann Lawton? In the play?

MISS LAND   Ann Lawton and Geoffrey Whittaker.

ALAN   Three times a week after school? Just Ann Lawton and me? And Geoffrey?

MISS LAND   You're going into a trance again, Duckworth, get out.

*He starts for the door, scarcely able to breathe with excitement. Suddenly he stops and starts pulling his socks up.*

MISS LAND   I thought I told you to get out?

ALAN   Yes, but before that you told me it's time I pulled my –

*She hurls a piece of chalk at his head.*

MISS LAND   Out!

*He hurries out.*

### 34  The corridor

*Alan emerges from the classroom and starts walking along the now-deserted corridor, hugging his copy of the play tightly to his bosom. Slowly, excitedly, (and, for the first time since we've met him) a smile begins to spread across his face.*

JOHN A   So Duckworth's in with a chance. The gods are smiling, the sun's shining, Quack-Quack's innings can now really begin. With the cheers of the crowd ringing in his ears, he makes his way to the wicket to try to win the match for England. To try to achieve the impossible.

*With the roar of the crowd ringing in his ears, Alan continues down the corridor to the exit.*

### 35  Waste ground

*A canal bank nearby. In the distance, factories, warehouses and railway depots. The waste ground is about as unlike a cricket pitch as it's possible to be. But, somehow, in the middle, a flat stretch serves the same purpose. There are three (different-sized) stumps at the batsman's end and a pile of jackets at the bowler's.*

*On it a group of boys are playing a scratch game of five-a-side. The bowler starts his run-up.*

JOHN A   And all Lords is hushed as Duckworth takes guard and faces his first ball from Keith Miller. And Miller races in, all fire and fury, and . . .

*Cut to Alan, batting. He hammers the ball high into the air.*

JOHN A   ... bowls ... And Duckworth hooks it heavens-high – a mighty, scything blow – clean out of the ground.

*Alan has, in fact, skied the ball out of sight. Everyone except him is dismayed.*

BOY 1   You gormless bugger!

BOY 2   It's in the bloody canal, you berk!

BOY 3   If it is, you're out.

ALAN   Decent shot, though, wasn't it?

BOY 3   A lost ball means you're six and out.

*They all troop off angrily to search for the ball. Alan, feeling immensely pleased with himself, wanders over to Shaz, who's sitting on some debris nearby, waiting for his turn. He's reading 'The Tables Turned'.*

SHAZ   (*without looking up from the page*) We'll have to move that canal.

ALAN   Decent shot, though, wasn't it? Meat of the bat behind it and everything. Crack! That was his chinaman, as well. I detected it in flight. It was all footwork, really – back on my right foot, then crack!

SHAZ   (*abruptly, blankly, still reading*) You've got to kiss her!

ALAN   (*blankly*) What?

SHAZ   (*looking up at Alan, twisting his face in amused disgust and making wet kissing noises*) You've to bloody kiss her!!

ALAN   Who?

SHAZ   (*reads aloud*) 'Antoine dismisses Rowlands with a confident smile. Antoine: "Never again will I tread that path. I've seen the light, Rowlands. The light of truth in what's happened. And the light of love in your fiancée's eyes. Love for *me*!" He strides towards Lady Daphne, takes her in his arms and *kisses* her ...' (*He boggles at Alan*) Ann Lawton's playing Lady Daphne, is she?

*Alan just stares at him.*

SHAZ   Well, you've to bloody kiss her!!

*Alan swallows. There have been many sentences uttered since the Creation of Man. Of all of them – to Alan's ears – that just uttered by Shaz is the most beautiful.*

ALAN (*with painfully-attempted nonchalance*) Have I?

ABBOT (*utterly disgusted, reading the same passage*) '. . . takes her into his arms and kisses her. Antoine: "And with that kiss you are mine – and I no longer a philanderer." Curtain.' Uuuggghh! Not with Smelly Lawton . . . !

ALAN They can't make me.

SHAZ It's in black and white, squire!

ALAN (*with attempted resignation*) Just my sodding luck . . .

BOY 1 (*calling*) Found it!

ALAN (*calling back*) I'm not out, then! Come on!

*The other boys are all trooping back from the canal bank. Alan turns to Shaz. Beams euphorically.*

ALAN I'll get a hundred tonight, you watch! How many am I now?

SHAZ Seven.

ALAN I'll get a bloody hundred!

*He runs back into position, brandishing his bat, happy and confident.*

JOHN A And Duckworth, brandishing his bat, means business. Miller, looking a little subdued, runs up, bowls . . . And Duckworth contemptuously clouts it through mid-off.

## 36 Alan's bedroom (night)

*Alan is in bed, reading the play, bursting with happiness and excitement.*

ALAN (*reading aloud*) 'I've seen the light, Rowlands. The light of truth in what's happened. And the light of love in your fiancée's eyes. Love for *me*!! (*He swallows*) 'Antoine strides towards Lady Daphne, takes her in his arms and kisses her.' (*Swallow again*) 'Antoine strides towards Lady Daphne, takes her in his arms and – ' (*Drops the book*) Oh, God, oh, God! He takes her in his arms and –

*He lies staring at the ceiling for a moment. Then suddenly leaps out of bed and starts getting dressed.*

## 37 The street (night)

*Alan races down the street, 'bowling' occasionally as he goes.*

### 38 Inside the fish and chip shop

*The proprietor is finishing serving a customer. Alan races in and stands panting at the counter.*

ALAN  Is anything ready – or is it still cooking – whatisit – frying . . .

PROPRIETOR  By hell, the Wanderer returns! I thought you must've gone into hibernation or something . . .

ALAN  No . . . er . . . can I have three fish and –

PROPRIETOR  I thought, either that or he's emigrated . . . It's not normal, I thought, all these weeks without . . .

ALAN  Um . . . three fish and three lots of chips, please. Salt and vinegar. All in the same bag.

PROPRIETOR  Sorry?

ALAN  All in one together. Chippiness lumpdom.

PROPRIETOR  Sorry?

ALAN  Triple amalgamatory edibleness.

*Pause.*

PROPRIETOR  (*drily*) No need to worry, had I? You're as normal as ever . . .

### 39 The street

*Alan strolls contentedly back towards his house, wolfing his three portions of fish and chips.*

### 40 Alan's house

*Alan throws the empty chip paper away and goes into his house.*

MOTHER  Alan! Where've you . . . (*Pause*) You smell of vinegar.

ALAN  I felt peckish.

MOTHER  There were four sausage rolls over from tea-time.

ALAN  I'll have them as well.

### 41 The school hall

*Late afternoon. The hall is empty apart from two cleaners at work – and Miss Land, Alan, Geoffrey and Ann onstage.*

*Miss Land stands behind a small trestle-table directing the play. Alan, Geoffrey and Ann are dotted randomly about. All have a copy of the play in their hands.*

ANN  (*reading*) My fiancée tells me that you are a stranger to St Albans, Mr Coveney.

ALAN  (*reading: to his boots*) I'd be grateful if you'd call me Antoine, my dear.

MISS LAND  Duckworth, you're mumbling.

ALAN  (*shouting*) I'd be grateful if you'd call me Antoine, my dear!

MISS LAND  She's not in Australia, Duckworth. Try half-way. Madagascar.

ALAN  (*stiltedly; but not quite so loudly*) I'd be grateful if you'd call me Antoine, my dear.

ANN  Calling you Antoine might be deemed a little familiar, Mr Coveney. *You* calling me 'my dear' is excessively so!

MISS LAND  (*reading stage directions*) She storms from the drawing room. (*Ann starts meandering off, her finger in her mouth.*) 'Storms', Ann, not shuffles. And people don't storm anywhere while sucking their finger.

ANN  I was just trying to push the skin down, Miss, to make the cuticle bigger.

MISS LAND  Are big cuticles in the play?

ANN  (*puzzled*) No . . . In real *life*, Miss.

MISS LAND  Ann. Please storm from the drawing room as the author requires.

*Ann comes back centre-stage, then storms off again. Then returns.*

MISS LAND  Thank you. (*To Alan*) Continue.

ALAN  (*reading*) I fear your intended is somewhat displeased with me, Rowlands. She appears –

MISS LAND  Duckworth! Number one: say the line to Geoffrey, not your armpit. And number two: the fact that she's displeased with you is immaterial to you. You're a philanderer. A grown man. A man of the world. You're *amused* that she's upset.

ALAN  (*puzzled*) That doesn't make sense, Miss.

MISS LAND  Perfect sense, Duckworth! That's precisely what grown men are *like*! It's extremely perceptive writing! Proceed.

ALAN  (*with an appalling attempt at being amused*) I fear your intended is somewhat displeased with me, Rowlands.

*There's a silence.*

MISS LAND  (*to Geoffrey*) Well?

GEOFFREY  (*suddenly realising it's his turn*) Oh, sorry. Um . . . (*reading*) I suggest you leave St Albans on the morning charabanc, Coveney. I know of your notorious, nay, nefarious exploits in London. I know of the safes you have robbed of diamonds. Of the ladies you have robbed of repute. Of the hearts you have robbed of happiness.

ALAN    *(acting 'scornful')* Ha, ha!

MISS LAND    Good. Now, as well as laughing scornfully, Duckworth, if you could – *(She involuntarily utters a small yelp)* Oh!

*They all look at her. For a brief moment, she seems to be in extreme discomfort – then gradually her face grows more and more bathed in overjoyed relief. A long pause.*

MISS LAND    *(happily)* Um ... look ... sorry about this ... I'm suddenly not feeling too well ... not well at all ... I'm sorry to say. So we'll stop rehearsal there – and carry on on Wednesday ... so, if you'll all excuse me.

*She runs off, in delight. The others watch her, puzzled.*

## 42 A street corner (later that afternoon)

*Ann, Geoffrey and Alan are walking home from the rehearsal and approaching the corner. Ann is in between the two boys.*

ALAN    Well, in my considered opinion, it'll be 159 years before we're ready to act it in front of the whole school ...

GEOFFREY    Today was a short rehearsal, that's all. We'll be OK.

ALAN    159 years minimum.

ANN    *(irritated)* You do *drip*, don't you!

ALAN    No?

ANN    Not much!

GEOFFREY    I think we're doing hot-diggity-dog.

ANN    *(confidently)* I do.

*They walk along in silence for a moment.*

GEOFFREY    By Wednesday I'm going to know the first scene by heart.

ANN    *I* am.

ALAN    Me too.

*Another short silence. They reach the corner, where Geoffrey goes his separate way.*

GEOFFREY    See you on the morrow, then.

ANN    Cert.

GEOFFREY    Unless you want to go train-spotting tonight ... or anything ...

ANN   I'm learning my part.

GEOFFREY   Oh, yes. (*He turns off towards his home, then looks back at Alan*) Don't you go *that* way? (*He points*)

ALAN   I've an errand to do for my dad. Paternal jobosity.

GEOFFREY   Where?

ALAN   Palmerston Avenue way.

ANN   *I* live down Palmerston.

ALAN   (*innocently*) Oh.

GEOFFREY   See you then.

ALAN   P'tang, yang, kipperbang, uuh!

GEOFFREY   (*pained*) I don't *do* P'tang, yang, kipperbang.

ALAN   Oh. Sorry.

GEOFFREY   (*to Ann, slightly embarrassed by Alan's presence*) Mañana.

ANN   (*also slightly embarrassed*) Mañana.

GEOFFREY
and ANN   Mañana's not soon enough for me.

*Alan is equally embarrassed. Geoffrey departs. Alan and Ann walk along together.*

ANN   I loathe and detest all that 'paternal jobosity' drivel.

ALAN   Pardon?

ANN   You and your crackpot pals. Long, stupid words that don't mean anything. 'Crepuscular dimension', 'incandescent geophydom' . . .

ALAN   It's only in fun. It's a joke. Jocularity undimini –

*He stops short on getting a dirty look from her. They walk on.*

### 43 Palmerston Avenue (a few minutes later)

*Alan and Ann are walking along in silence. Alan's racking his brains, trying to think of something to talk about without irritating her.*

ALAN   I wasn't really dripping. All I meant was we're only on page 4.

ANN   It was our first rehearsal.

ALAN   Yes. Yes, granted. It was. Definitely. (*Pause*) But there's 51 pages altogether . . . before we get to the end.

ANN   So what?

ALAN   Just that I'll be happier when we're on page 51.

ANN   You just want it over with.

ALAN   No . . . just to be on the last page, that's all . . .

ANN    And I know why.

ALAN   (*guiltily, embarrassed*) Do you?

ANN    Of course I do. It's perfectly obvious. (*Pause*) Because you're a drip.

*She goes into her house. He continues down the street until he's sure she's closed the door, then executes his immediate about-turn and starts returning the way he came.*

JOHN A    And Duckworth looks in trouble yet again. And as the teams go in for tea, there's precious little going right for him. Every time he's about to get a grip on the game, Lindwall seems to have the last word. Disconsolate now, discouraged, deeply depressed at the immensity of his task, he trudges back to the pavilion. But, surely, he must take heart that he's still not out ... that he still has the chance to grit his teeth ... and try again.

## 44  Inside the cricket pavilion (night)

*Tommy and Miss Land are facing each other – each gripping the other excitedly by the elbows – their faces bright with joy and overwhelming relief.*

TOMMY    Are you sure??

MISS LAND    (*grinning like a clown*) Don't I look it!!

TOMMY    Oh, Miss Land!

MISS LAND    (*bubbling over into euphoric laughter*) Oh, God ... I'd forgotten what it was like to laugh!

TOMMY    (*hugging her in delight*) I feel so ... I feel ... I don't know what to do with myself I feel so ...

MISS LAND    Oh, me too! The relief! The sheer ... Oh, God, thank you ... It's all over ... now we can stop seeing each other ...

TOMMY    (*happily*) Never see each other again!

MISS LAND    Oh, Tommy ... all over ... it's all over ... I don't know whether to sing or dance or ...

*She subsides, laughing into his arms. They kiss through their laughter. The kisses grow more urgent. Caresses become grappling. They sink to the floor, passionately fumbling with clothing. The laughter turns to heavy breathing. Out of sheer relief, they're about to do it again.*

### 45 From outside the cricket pavilion (a few moments later)

*The light shines from the window. After a moment, it's switched off.*

MISS LAND   Are you free Sunday night?

TOMMY   Won't you be at Evensong?

MISS LAND   *After* Evensong . . .

TOMMY   Oh, Miss Land . . .!


### 46 The school hall (late afternoon)

*The new, happy and bright Miss Land is at her trestle table directing Alan, Ann and Geoffrey, who still clutch their copies of the play.*

MISS LAND   Very good. (*To Alan*) Whereupon you dismiss him with a confident smile.

*Alan smiles weakly at Geoffrey.*

MISS LAND   A confident one, Duckworth. Do you know how to be confident? I think the author would like it. (*Alan performs another feeble smile*) Is that it? I see. Well, the author will have to be disappointed. Alright, Whittaker, consider yourself dismissed with a confident smile. Continue, Duckworth.

ALAN   (*reading*) Never again will I tread that path. I've seen the light, Rowlands. The light of truth in what's happened. And the light of –

MISS LAND   Turn to Lady Daphne.

ALAN   (*turning to Ann*) . . . And the light of love in your fiancée's eyes. Love for *me*.

MISS LAND   And walk towards her. (*He does so*) Good. (*Then, rapidly winding the proceedings up*) At which point you take-her-in-your-arms-kiss-her-do-the-last-line-about-now-she's-yours-and-you're-no-longer-a-philanderer. Good! Rehearsal again on Friday, four o'clock.

ALAN   (*gaping at her blankly*) Um . . .

MISS LAND   Yes, Duckworth?

ALAN   Aren't we going to actually . . .

*He glances for support to Ann and Geoffrey, but they're busily gathering their satchels and belongings, ready to leave.*

MISS LAND   To actually *what*, Duckworth? It's five o'clock.

ALAN   Ah . . . No, it's alright, then . . . It doesn't matter . . .

### 47 The waste ground (evening)

*A scratch five-a-side cricket match has been halted, while the same group of boys from school are once again searching the canal bank for a lost ball.*

*Alan, Shaz and Abbo are seated on the pile of debris. Shaz, who's the one who's lost the ball, still holds the bat. Abbo is holding Alan's copy of the school play – testing Alan on his lines.*

ABBO 'What the devil do you mean, you blackguard?'

ALAN 'Precisely what you fear I mean, sir. I have been searching the earth for its most precious diamond and found it here. Er, not in Lady Daphne's necklace, but in her heart.'

ABBO 'He dismisses him with a confident smile.'

ALAN 'Um ... I've seen the light, Rowlands.'

ABBO You've missed a sentence out. 'I will never tread that path again.'

ALAN Oh yes. 'I will never tread that path again. I have seen the light, Rowlands. The light of love –'

ABBO *(correcting him)* The light of *truth.*

ALAN Oh, yes. 'The light of truth in what's happened. And the light of love in your fiancée's eyes. Love for *me.*'

*Immediate heckling from Shaz and Abbo.*

ABBO *(reading)* Then you stride over to her, take her in your arms and *(He loudly and grotesquely mimes being sick)*

SHAZ Pukedom vomitudinosity!

ABBO Spewosity upthrow.

ALAN *(violently)* That's stupid, that!! *(They stare at him in bewilderment)* Long, drivel words that don't mean anything! It's crackpot talk!

*He snatches the book away from him, then walks away. An uncomfortable silence. Shaz and Abbo look at each other, puzzled and troubled.*

SHAZ He's getting more like my Auntie Phyllis every day.

ABBO It's the strain of learning his lines.

SHAZ Either that, or he's been overdoing it.

ABBO Overdoing it can't make you go like your Auntie Phyllis, can it?

### 48 The school hall (late afternoon)

*Miss Land, Alan, Ann and Geoffrey are rehearsing as before, still using their books.*

ALAN   And the light of love in your fiancée's eyes. Love for *me*.

*He walks towards Ann as though in a trance. Heart pounding, he takes her in his arms. He's finally about to kiss her. At the last moment, he suddenly starts drying his lips on the back of his hand. Miss Land watches, bemused.*

MISS LAND   What on earth are you doing?

ALAN   (*hoarsely*) Drying my lips, Miss.

MISS LAND   Well, don't! There's something faintly not very nice about it. Just kiss her. With your ordinary lips.

ALAN   (*puzzled*) When they're dry it makes them more bare.

MISS LAND   Just kiss her!

ALAN   Yes, Miss.

*He takes Ann in his arms again – about to kiss her – then . . .*

GEOFFREY   (*raising his hand*) Please, Miss?

MISS LAND   Yes, Whittaker?

GEOFFREY   You said I could go early today, Miss, owing to three fillings at the dentist's.

MISS LAND   Quite right, so I did. (*Claps hands to end the rehearsal*) Off you pop, everyone. Hometime.

ALAN   (*heart sinking*) But, Miss!

MISS LAND   Complaining again, Duckworth?

ALAN   *We're* still here, Miss! Miss, we've never done this last bit, Miss!

MISS LAND   We'll be doing it on Monday, Duckworth. For our sins.

ALAN   But that's the day itself, Miss! The real thing!

MISS LAND   That's right, Duckworth.

JOHN A   Now, this really is becoming quite uncanny. Once more, Duckworth, is left frustrated and forlorn at the wicket. Just as he was shaping up for a match-winning six, the umpires have stopped play for bad light. *He's* obviously prepared to play on till midnight. But the Aussies are trouping off the pitch . . . and so now is Duckworth, still determined, though a little desperately, one suspects . . . to stay in the game.

### 49 The street corner (later that afternoon)

*Geoffrey, Ann and Alan are on their way home from rehearsal.*

GEOFFREY See you, then.

ANN Hope it all goes hot-diggity at the dentist's.

GEOFFREY Cert. Mañana.

ANN Mañana.

GEOFFREY
and ANN Mañana's not soon enough for me.

*Geoffrey realises that, once again, Alan is making no attempt to move. He looks at him levelly, accusingly.*

GEOFFREY You going on an errand for your dad again, are you?

ALAN Definitely.

GEOFFREY You go a *lot* of errands for your dad, don't you? Down Palmerston.

ALAN (*shrugs*) A fair amount.

GEOFFREY (*firmly to Ann for Alan's benefit*) See you outside the Odeon, Saturday.

*He strides off, irritated. Ann starts off towards her house. Alan goes with her.*

### 50 Palmerston Avenue (a few moments later)

*Alan and Ann walking towards Ann's house. Once again Alan racks his brains for intelligent – but uncontroversial – conversation.*

ALAN In my considered opinion, Antoine probably wanted to kiss Lady Daphne right at the start, when he first –

ANN No, he didn't. At the start all he wants to do is pinch her jewellery!

ALAN (*realising he's in trouble again. Back-pedals, trying to wriggle out*) Yes ... yes, he does ... but when he discovers it's *Rowlands* who's the *real* criminal ... and to, you know, save her from his vile clutches ... I think what he does is dream of the moment when –

ANN Quack-Quack! Antoine Coveney's a real *man*. Lady Daphne's but a mere woman. He does whatever he *wants* to do! Just *does* it! No messing!

ALAN (*defeated*) Definitely.

ANN   *Real* men don't mess about *dreaming.*

ALAN  No.

*She goes into her house. Alan continues some little way past, then does his customary about-turn. As he does so, he catches sight of Ann watching him through her hall window. He promptly – all in the same movement – turns his about-turn into another about-turn; and resumes walking down the street in precisely the opposite direction to the one he wants to take.*

## 51  Alan's bedroom (night)

*Alan is standing facing the mirror, wearing pyjama trousers.*

ALAN  (*into the mirror*) And the light of love in your fiancée's eyes. Love for *me.*

*He walks closer to the mirror, arms extended. They embrace an imaginary Ann. He inclines his head to kiss her – then stops to rub his lips dry with the back of his hand – then starts again. Just as he's about to kiss . . . .*

MOTHER  Alan! What's your dinner doing in the dog's bowl?

*He immediately – guiltily – jumps away from the imaginary embrace.*

MOTHER  Are you starting your Mahatma Gandhi again?

*Alan sighs, and gets into bed.*

JOHN A  So then, with England so near and yet so far, play is interrupted yet again. The news, paddled over the puddles from the pavilion, is that the umpires will inspect the wicket at one-thirty, if there's no more rain before lunch. In which case, play will resume at two . . . unless, of course, there's rain between one-thirty and two. In which case, they'll inspect the wicket at three. So, once again . . . and quite rightly too . . . the answer lies in the heavens.

## 52  The school corridor (day)

*Classroom doors open. Each class of kids emerges, shepherded by teachers down the corridor to the main hall.*

### 53 The school hall

*The kids stream noisily in, to be settled in their seats by their teachers. Much chatter, scraping of chairs, cuffs round the ears by the teachers. Backstage, we hear a gramophone – slowly beginning to wind down.*

### 54 'The wings' of the stage

*Miss Land is frantically winding up a gramophone. The music resumes its proper speed.*

*Beside her, Alan, Ann and Geoffrey are putting the final touches to their appearance and costumes. The play is set in 1930. Alan now sports a big moustache; and Geoffrey an ill-fitting grey wig. Ann is incongruously wearing a ball-gown. All four are in a state of nervous collapse.*

*Alan glances at Ann. She looks beautiful. He half-smiles at her – a smile of trembling excitement. She looks away.*

### 55 The school hall (a few minutes later)

*The entire school is now seated. On the front row are the Headmaster and staff (apart from Miss Land).*

*Gradually the noise subsides as the music from the gramophone reaches a crescendo.*

*The curtains part to reveal onstage an extremely amateurish and artificial drawing room of a county manor near St Albans.*

*Ann is centre-stage, arranging flowers in a bowl. This gives rise to a few giggles from her classmates, a smattering of applause, a couple of subdued catcalls – and frosty looks from the teachers of the culprits.*

### 56 'The wings'

*Miss Land, Alan and Geoffrey are watching Ann onstage.*
MISS LAND (*suddenly*) Now!

*She pushes Geoffrey onto the stage.*

### 57 The school hall

*Geoffrey appears onstage – a little more quickly than he would have without being pushed.*

*The sight of his wig is greeted with more (subdued) catcalls and laughter. The culprits are mostly the boys of 4B. The teachers silence them with a look.*

GEOFFREY  Good afternoon, Daphne.

ANN  Charles, dearest! I didn't expect you till tea-time.

GEOFFREY  I know, my dear. But this is more than a visit from a doting fiancé – (*Catcalls from 4B, frostily silenced by teachers*) – As you know, I am Chief Magistrate for St Albans . . .

### 58 'The wings'

*Miss Land and Alan stand, both mouthing Ann's words as we hear –*

ANN  A pillar of our society, Charles. The whole of Hertfordshire respects you. I, for my part, respect you – and *more*.

### 59 The school hall

*Giggles from the junior girls at Ann's last line.*

GEOFFREY  Thank you, dearest. Well, in my official capacity, the police have informed me that an unscrupulous criminal from London has been seen motoring in his Alvis Coupé up the A1. A gentleman diamond-thief . . . notorious for winning the hearts of ladies only to steal their jewels.

### 60 'The wings'

*Miss Land presses the button of a chiming doorbell.*

### 61 The school hall

*Ann 'jumps' on hearing the chimes.*

ANN  Goodness me, Charles, you've made me jumpy! I wonder who that can be . . . ?

### 62 Outside the school

*A police car drives down the road and turns into the school drive-way. It stops at the main entrance of the school building. Two policemen get out and go into the school.*

### 63 The school hall

*Ann is still onstage. Geoffrey re-enters.*

GEOFFREY It's a chap whose car's broken down outside the Manor. Seems a decent sort of cove. I said he could join us while I telephone a garage for him. Ah, here he is now.

*Alan enters, almost frozen in fear. Immediate howls of laughter from the boys of 4B.*

SHAZ/ABBO (*with appropriate hand-gesture*) P'tang, yang, kipperbang, uuh!

*A teacher shuts them up.*

GEOFFREY May I introduce you to my fiancée, the Honourable Lady Daphne.

ALAN Charmed to make your acquaintance, Lady Daphne. What a delightful home you have.

ANN Thank you. Have you many friends in these parts?

ALAN The Hertfordshire Caldicotts were old friends of my family till their return to Pretoria. Colonel Caldicott and I shot grouse together in Scotland.

### 64 The school hall

*Cut to the (elderly) school secretary entering the hall. She hurriedly makes her way to the Headmaster who is asleep on the front row, and wakes him.*

*He applauds thinking the play is over. She whispers in his ear. He seems puzzled. He gets up and hurries from the hall.*

### 65 Outside the school buildings (a few minutes later)

*Two policemen are waiting by their car as the Headmaster and school secretary hurry out.*

HEAD Now, what can I do for you, Sergeant?

SERGEANT I'm, er, making some enquiries, sir.

### 66 The cricket pavilion

*Tommy, whistling happily – which is something we've never seen him do before – is busy with some maintenance work.*

*He glances up – to see the Headmaster and the two policemen coming out of the school entrance. The headmaster points in Tommy's direction. Tommy immediately stops whistling.*

*He watches, warily, suspiciously, as the two policemen thank the Headmaster and start to make their way across the sports field towards Tommy.*

## 67 The school hall (a few minutes later)

*Onstage, Alan, Geoffrey and Ann are now seated 'drinking' tea.*

GEOFFREY  Goodness me! So pleasant and urbane has been our conversation, that I quite forgot to telephone the garage for you! (*He goes to a 'phone*) What make of car have you, Mr Coveney?

ALAN  It's an Alvis. An Alvis Coupé.

*Ann and Geoffrey 'act' shocked reaction.*

## 68 The cricket pavilion

*From the point of view of the Headmaster (standing, worriedly, at the school entrance) we see the two policemen talking to Tommy outside the pavilion.*

*One of them is taking notes. Tommy seems deeply agitated.*

*Finally, one of the policemen takes his arm, and they both start to escort him to the police car.*

## 69 The school hall (later)

*Alan, Ann and Geoffrey onstage – now reaching the end of the play.*

ALAN  I've seen the light, Rowlands. The light of truth in what's happening. And the light of love in your fiancée's eyes. Love for *me*!

*This is it. The moment has finally arrived. The moment when Alan's dreams become reality. The moment his prayer is to be granted. The moment of The Kiss.*

*Alan walks slowly towards Ann.*

JOHN A  Now, let's try and be calm about this. England are just one run short of the greatest victory of all time. Young Duckworth, 364 not out, has equalled Len Hutton's world record.

*Alan looks into Ann's eyes. She looks beautiful. He moves to take her in his arms.*

JOHN A   And now he's facing the very last ball of the match.

*Alan inclines his head to kiss Ann.*

JOHN A   And Lindwall bowls it!

*Alan glances at the audience. One by one, he sees Shaz, Abbo and others from his class. All staring at him.*
  *He looks back at Ann: her lips ready pursed, her eyes closed.*

JOHN A   And Duckworth ...

*We see their faces: Abbo's, Shaz's, Alan's, Geoffrey's, Ann's.*

JOHN A   And Duckworth ...

*As though in a trance, Alan drops his arms from the embrace and steps back a pace. Ann – bewildered – unpurses her lips and opens her eyes.*

JOHN A   And Duckworth ...

*With tears starting in his eyes, Alan solemnly shakes Ann by the hand.*
  *Ann is dumbstruck. So is Geoffrey, Abbo, Shaz and most of the audience. Dumbstruck almost to coma is Miss Land gaping at him from the wings.*

ALAN   *(trancelike)* For with that kiss, you are now mine – and I no longer a philanderer.

*Music from the gramophone. The curtains close. The audience watches in baffled silence for a moment, then gradually, and a little bemusedly, begins some vague applause.*

## 70  Outside the school buildings

*Tommy is seen sitting in the back of the police car. He looks up at the sound of the children's applause.*

## 71  'The wings'

*Alan, Ann and Geoffrey are taking off their make-up. Alan wants to die; Geoffrey is revelling in Alan's discomfiture; Miss Land is livid. Ann watches Alan, in puzzled concern.*

MISS LAND (*yelling at Alan*) Ruined! Completely ruined! Weeks of rehearsals, the whole play in ashes! What on earth possessed you!!

GEOFFREY It's never like that with Stewart Grainger ... I mean, imagine Stewart Grainger seeing the light of love in Hedy Lamarr's eyes and just –

ANN Geoffrey, don't.

GEOFFREY – and just standing there like a twerp, shaking hands with her, while choirs of angels are –

ANN Stop it, Geoffrey.

MISS LAND (*to Alan*) If you never wanted to kiss her, you should have said so right at the start, and we'd have got someone who would have quite liked to! You're a mess and a weed and a lolloper, Duckworth! You lollop!

*The Headmaster pops his head round.*

HEAD Excuse me, Miss Land.

MISS LAND I'm sorry about the ending, Headmaster! Duckworth here deliberately –

HEAD If I may just borrow you for a moment.

*He beckons her outside.*


### 73 The corridor to the hall

*One of the policemen is standing waiting. The Headmaster ushers Miss Land through a door opening on the corridor. She stops, blankly, on seeing the policeman.*

MISS LAND Oh ...!

HEAD Miss Land ... Something's happened. It appears that young Tommy, the groundsman –

MISS LAND I don't know what you mean! He's nothing to do with ... I've hardly even ... whatever's been ...

HEAD It appears he was a deserter in the war. A deserter from the East Lanchashire Regiment.

POLICEMAN June 17th., 1943, Aldershot. Three weeks after he was called up.

*Miss Land stares from one to the other, in shock.*

HEAD And he's just been ... well, *arrested*, really ...

POLICEMAN To be handed over to a Military Police escort and taken for

Court Martial. He ... um ... he requested if I'd be kind enough to pass on a message to you, ma'am ...

MISS LAND  Why me? I've only ever said good morning or ...

POLICEMAN  Well, it's not for you in particular, ma'am.

MISS LAND  Sorry?

POLICEMAN  He said there's a boy in your class. Name of Duckworth. He said – (*reads from his notebook*) ... 'Whatever he hears, ask him not to think too bad of me owing to me not being the hero he thought I was.' (*Closes the notebook*) That's all, ma'am.

HEAD  The dichotomy of Appearance and Reality again, I suppose, Miss Land. The whole Shakespearean canon. (*To policeman by way of explanation*) Miss Land is our English expert.

POLICEMAN  (*puzzled*) Oh, yes?

HEAD  (*sighing*) I'll escort you to your car, Officer.

POLICEMAN  Thank you, sir.

*The Headmaster starts to trundle away. The policeman smiles sadly at Miss Land.*

POLICEMAN  Thank you, ma'am.

MISS LAND  (*sadly*) Thank *you*.

POLICEMAN  (*turns to go*) Not at all.

MISS LAND  Incidentally, Officer ... (*He turns back*) I'm a Miss not a Ma'am. (*Smiles levelly into his eyes*) For your information.

POLICEMAN  (*uncertainly*) Right, Miss.

*He goes. Miss Land watches him for a moment, lost in thought, then abruptly snaps out of it, and calls back to the wings.*

MISS LAND  Duckworth, come here!

### 73  A street corner (late afternoon)

*Geoffrey, Alan and Ann trudging home after the play. Slowly and in silence. Alan is sadly, gravely, preoccupied. Not, for a change, close to tears. Now somehow beyond tears. Ann keeps glancing at him, in concern and puzzlement. Geoffrey feels uncomfortably excluded.*

ANN  *Why*, though, Quack-Quack! Why didn't you do the kiss? You haven't said why.

*Alan barely shrugs in reply. She tries again – hopefully.*

ANN  Did you just forget?

GEOFFREY  He nearly forgot three whole *lines* on page 20. About may he look at your bracelet, owing to him being a jewellery expert, till I prompted him!

*He reaches the spot where they go their different ways.*

GEOFFREY  I'll say mañana, then.

ANN  (*to Alan*) I mean there must be a reason. Everything has a reason . . .

GEOFFREY  (*watching them warily*) I said 'I'll say mañana, then' . . .

ANN  (*to Alan*) You can walk me home if you like.

GEOFFREY  (*panicking a little*) Mañana.

ALAN  (*shrugs in reply to Ann's invitation*) Alright.

*They walk on, leaving Geoffrey staring helplessly after them.*

GEOFFREY  Mañana's not soon enough for me . . .

*They ignore him completely and go on their way.*

### 74 Palmerston Avenue (day)

*Alan and Ann walk on, as before.*

ANN  What do you *think* was the reason?˙

ALAN  I don't know.

ANN  (*trying to jolly him out of his mood*) You don't know much, then, do you!

ALAN  (*simply*) No. I don't. I know nothing. (*Pause*) I used to think I knew everything about everything. The world and that. But I don't. (*Pause*) Maybe I got it wrong.

ANN  Got *what* wrong?

ALAN  Everything. Tommy. The world. Maybe it's *all* lies.

ANN  What is?

ALAN  Everything I thought. About everything.

*She looks at him. He shivers, involuntarily.*

ANN  You're shivering.

ALAN  Yes.

ANN  Maybe you're sickening for something.

ALAN  Maybe.

*They walk on in silence. After a moment or two –*

ALAN  A few weeks ago I trod on a big, fat spider and hundreds of little ones came running out of it. I thought it was perhaps a miracle.

ANN   (*hotly*) I don't know about a miracle, it was sodding *cruel*!

ALAN   Accidental.

ANN   (*simmering down*) Oh. (*Pause*) It must just've been pregnant. You just gave it a sort of caesarean.

ALAN   Oh, I see.

ANN   I don't think it'll have been a miracle. It's just Nature, really.

ALAN   Yes.

ANN   Except Nature *is* a miracle, isn't it?

ALAN   (*stopping, looks at her, smiles – abeit a little sadly*) Yes. I forgot that. Yes it is. Supposedly.

*They're now at the gate of Ann's house. They stand for a moment in silence.*

ANN   Why didn't you want to kiss me? Am I that grotesque to the nth degree?

ALAN   (*looking at her. He speaks quietly solemnly, completely unselfconsciously, and very, very simply*) You're beautiful, Ann. Sometimes I look at you and you're so beautiful I want to cry. And sometimes you look so beautiful I want to laugh and jump up and down, and run through the streets with no clothes on shouting 'P'tang, yang, kipperbang' in people's letterboxes. (*Pause*) But mostly you're so beautiful – even if it doesn't make *me* cry it makes my chest cry. Your lips are the most beautiful. Second is your nape.

ANN   (*slight pause*) My what?

ALAN   The back of your neck. It's termed the nape.

ANN   Oh, my *nape*.

ALAN   And your skin. When I walk past your desk, I breathe in on purpose to smell your skin. It's the most beautiful smell there is.

ANN   It's only Yardley's.

ALAN   It makes me feel dizzy. Giddy. You smell brand-new. You look brand-new. All of you. The little soft hairs on your arms.

ANN   That's *down*. It's not hairs. It's called down. Girls can have down.

ALAN   But mostly it's your lips. I love your lips. That's why I've *always* wanted to kiss you. Ever since 3B. Just kiss. Not the other things. I don't want to do the other things to you.

(*Pause*) Well, I *do*. *All* the other things. Sometimes I want to do them so much I feel I'm – do you have violin lessons?

ANN (*thrown*) What?

ALAN On the violin.

ANN No. Just the recorder. Intermediate, Grade Two.

ALAN Well, on a violin there's the E string. That's the highest pitched and it's strung very tight and taut, and makes a kind of high, sweet scream. Well, sometimes I want you so much, that's what *I'm* like.

*A pause.*

ANN (*uncertainly*) Um . . . thank you.

ALAN I always wanted to tell you you were lovely. Personally, I always think it's dead weedy when Victor Mature – or whatisname – Stewart Grainger – or someone says a girl's lovely. But you are. (*Pause*) And I know girls think it's weedy when boys call them sweet. But you are. (*Pause*) I don't expect I'll ever kiss you now in my whole life. Or take you to the pictures. Or marry you and do the *other* things to you. But I'll never forget you. And how you made me feel. Even when I'm 51 or something.

*A long pause. Whatever else is happening in the street – cars passing, people coming home from work, little kids playing – is unnoticed by them.*

ANN (*quietly, gently*) Why didn't you kiss me, then?

ALAN It's like cricketers. Well, I mean, it *isn't* like cricketers. Cyril Washbrook or Denis Compton or any of them . . . They face the bowler – and there are thousands of people watching . . . their families and friends and all the Australian fielders and the umpires and John Arlott and thousands of total strangers. And they don't care. Just keep their eye on the ball and play their stroke. I don't know how they do it. I couldn't.

ANN (*pause*) Would you like to kiss me *now*?

*He shakes his head sadly.*

ANN No one's watching.

*He shakes his head again.*

ANN Why not?

*Her eyes looking into his, Ann starts drying her lips with the back of her hand. Gently, Alan takes her hand away from her lips and holds it by his side. He smiles tenderly at her. A long moment. Then sadly shakes his head.*

ALAN  I'm sorry, Ann. It's too late.

ANN  (*tears starting into her eyes*) It isn't even five o'clock!

ALAN  I didn't mean that. Things are different now.

ANN  Why? What things??

ALAN  You were right, you see, Ann. *Real* men *don't* mess about dreaming. I *could* kiss you ... but it won't be like I dreamed it'd be. I know it won't. Nothing is. Kids kid themselves.

*A pause.*

ANN  (*hotly*) I think you won't kiss me because I said you *could*!

ALAN  What?

ANN  Because now I *want* you to.

ALAN  (*thrown; troubled*) Is that what happens?

ANN  I think you're just being sodding cruel again! Only this time on *purpose*!

ALAN  Don't cry, Ann. *I* used to cry. Even in my sleep ... dreaming. I won't any more, though. I've jacked in crying now.

*Ann looks into his eyes, bites back tears. Smiles sadly.*

ANN  Would you like to say P'tang, yang, kipperbang?

*He smiles; shakes his head.*

ANN  My favourite words are yellow ochre, burnt sienna and crimson lake.

ALAN  Very nice. (*Pause*) See you tomorrow.

*He turns to go.*

ANN  Alan?

*He turns back. She kisses him, very briefly, on the cheek.*

ANN  For good luck, that's all.

*He smiles and starts back down the street. She watches him go for a moment, then turns and goes into her house.*

### 75 Alan's street (a little later)

*Alan is walking towards his house. Gradually his gait is beginning to change ... becoming more confident ... then cocky ... than a downright swagger. He starts to grin to himself.*

JOHN A And Duckworth ... and · Duckworth ... and Duckworth has done it! He glances the ball calmly past fine short leg for a single. England have won the most dramatic victory in the history of cricket. And for the record-breaking 365 not out that won it, the entire crowd and I'll wager the entire nation, rises to its feet in homage to Quack-Quack Duckworth. Who went to the wicket a boy ... and came back a man.

*Alan passes the two workmen as they are about to climb into their lorry at the end of their days work. He nods to them curtly – the greeting of a man among men. They nod back in the same way. Alan goes into his house. They watch him go, impressed, despite themselves.*

WORKMAN 1 He'll be starting shaving next.

WORKMAN 2 Then spend the rest of his life trying to stop the bleeding.

*They drive off down the street.*

The next four pages show photographs from the TV production of *P'tang, Yang, Kipperbang*.

# Polly, Put the Kettle On

## The Cast

Polly, *bride's mother*
Duggie, *bride's father*
Christine, *bride*
Warren, *bridegroom*
Brian, *best man*
Shirley
Barbara } *bridesmaids*
Harry Chadwick, *Quartet leader*
Mr Toby, *head waiter*
Madge, *waitress*
Carol, *waitress*
Queenie, *washer-upper*
Alice
Old Tom Abbot
Uncle Stan
Aunt Dora
Drummer

3rd musician
4th musician
Denise
Ronnie, *Denise's husband*
Tracy, *Denise's daughter*
Poor Auntie Edna
Marion
Mr Lee
Mrs Edwards
Gladys
Jimmy
1st Guest
Vicar
Photographer
Taxi-driver, *non-speaking*
Marion's husband, *non-speaking*

# Polly, Put the Kettle On

## 1 Inside the church

*A small C. of E. church in a working-class district of London. As the play opens, the Vicar is partway through the marriage ceremony. Standing before him are the bride and groom, Christine and Warren; both of them, there against their will, are bored and irritated.*

*Beside Christine is her father, Duggie, standing to attention as he does when representing his union members in discussions with the management. His new collar is hurting a bit, and he wriggles his nose from time to time, to try and stop it itching without actually scratching it.*

*Beside Warren is the best man, Brian, winking from time to time at one of the bridesmaids, Barbara, who ignores him. The other bridesmaid, Shirley, keeps smiling at him – but he ignores her.*

*In the front pew is Polly, the bride's mother. This is the greatest day of her life. She's overdressed, over-excited and completely carried away by an awe and solemnity of occasion that isn't really there.*

VICAR Who giveth this woman to be married to this man?
DUGGIE Here. Um ... yes. Me.

*The Vicar takes Christine's hand and places it in Warren's.*

VICAR (*to Warren*) Now say after me ... I, Darren, take thee ...
WARREN (*interrupting*) Warren.
VICAR Sorry?
WARREN Warren, not Darren.
VICAR Ah. (*Resuming*) I, Warren, take thee, Christine, to my wedded wife ...
WARREN (*bored*) I, Warren, take thee, Christine to my wedded wife ...

*Throughout the recitation of the vows, the camera shows us as many as possible of the wedding guests; some of them looking at their watches, others looking around them to see who's been invited, a little girl picking her nose and being quietly clouted for it by her mother ...*

65

VICAR To have and to hold.

WARREN To have and to hold.

VICAR From this day forward.

WARREN From this day forward.

VICAR For better, for worse.

WARREN For better, for worse.

VICAR For richer, for poorer.

WARREN For richer, for poorer.

VICAR In sickness and in health.

WARREN In sickness and in health.

VICAR To love and to cherish.

WARREN To love and to cherish.

VICAR Till death us do part, according to God's holy ordinance.

WARREN Till death us do part, according to God's holy ordinance.

VICAR And thereto I plight thee my troth.

WARREN And thereto I plight thee my troth.

VICAR Very nice. (*He turns to Christine*) Now say after me . . . I Christine, take thee, Warren, to my wedded husband . . .

*Throughout the rest of Christine's recitation of her marriage vows the camera stays on Polly mouthing the responses, moved, intense, and solemn.*

VICAR To have and to hold.

CHRISTINE To have and to hold.

VICAR From this day forward.

CHRISTINE From this day forward.

VICAR For better, for worse.

CHRISTINE For better, for worse.

VICAR For richer, for poorer.

CHRISTINE For richer, for poorer.

VICAR In sickness and in health.

CHRISTINE In sickness and in health.

VICAR To love and to cherish.

CHRISTINE To love and to cherish.

*Polly adds the mouthed words 'and obey'*

VICAR Till death us do part, according to God's holy ordinance.

CHRISTINE Till death us do part, according to God's holy ordinance.

VICAR And thereto I give thee my troth.

CHRISTINE And thereto I give thee my troth.

*The Vicar takes the ring, hands it to Warren and helps him place it on Chrisine's finger.*
*Polly cranes forward so as not to miss a thing.*

## 2  Outside the church door

*Sheltering in the doorway from a heavy downfall of snow are the wedding photographer, cameras slung round his neck, yawning and flicking disinterestedly through the morning paper: and a wedding taxi-driver, also fed up, listening to a racing commentary on his transistor radio. The photographer glances at his watch.*

## 3  Inside the church

*The Vicar is addressing the congregation.*
*Throughout, concentrate on Polly, nodding her head in agreement with each phrase.*

VICAR  Forasmuch as Warren and Christine have consented together in holy wedlock, and have witnessed the same before God and this company, and thereto have given and pledged their troth either to the other, and have declared the same by giving and receiving of a ring and by joining of hands: I pronounce that they be Man and Wife together.

POLLY  *(before he can say another word)* Amen!!

## 4  Inside the Co-op hall kitchens

*We immediately cut to the sight of a stock of plates slipping from the hands of a young waitress, Carol, and smashing and shattering all over the floor. Cut from the reaction of Carol, herself, shocked and apologetic, to those of her fellow waitress, Madge, who's middle-aged, Queenie, an elderly and infirm washer-upper, Mr Toby, the head-waiter, who makes a career out of being long-suffering, and the members of the 'Four Aces in Harmony Quartet' who are standing at the other end of the kitchen, dressed in obsolete, tight, shiny, threadbare evening suits.*

*Cries from the quartet of 'Olé!', 'Having a smashing time?' and 'Nice one, Cyril!', etc.*

*Throughout the scene, as in all the kitchen scenes we hear the muted sounds from the Reception Room. In this case, the droning of speeches and occasional laughter and applause.*

CAROL    Trust me . . .

MR TOBY    Trust you!!

CAROL    And I was doing really great so far, wasn't I? Ten out of ten . . .

MR TOBY    Get it swept up, Carol.

CAROL    Yes Mr Toby. And I'd been a credit to the kitchen so far, hadn't I? All through the cream of tomato soup, and the . . .

MR TOBY    You spilt *two* plates of the cream of tomato, to *my* certain knowledge!

CAROL    Yeah, well, them apart . . . All through the ham salad and the ice-cream meringue . . .

MR TOBY    (*turning to look at Madge and Queenie who've stopped work to watch the discussion*) Well, carry on with your work! No one's proclaimed a national bloody holiday!

CAROL    I can hardly carry on with mine, can I? Mine's all over the lino.

MR TOBY    Madge, help her clear it up.

MADGE    *She* broke them.

MR TOBY    No one said she didn't.

MADGE    I'm supposed to be making fresh coffee.

MR TOBY    It'll wait a few minutes. They're not halfway through the speeches yet. (*He cocks his ear to listen to the sounds from the Reception Room – then suddenly realises what Madge has just said. He turns back to her in alarm*) What do you mean *fresh* coffee???

MADGE    Well, the same *coffee*. Fresh *water*.

MR TOBY    (*relaxing again*) Thank you. (*He resumes checking the liqueur bottles*) You'll give me a heart attack one day . . . shocks like that . . .

## 5  The reception room

*Duggie is midway through his speech. Polly is sitting beside him, beaming at the guests throughout and hanging on his every word. (From now until the wedding reception comes to an end, beneath Polly's relentless enjoyment of the occasion is a nervous undercurrent – an almost hysterical intensity to enjoy herself.)*

*Christine and Warren are bored stiff, irritable and fidgety.*

*(The entire wedding party were caught in a snow shower after leaving church. The men's hair and shoulders, and the ladies' hats are still flaked with snow.)*

DUGGIE    . . . and how pleased we are that so many of you have braved the elements and come all this way – from as far afield as Woolwich, East Acton, Crouch End, Battersea, and in some cases, Potters Bar – despite the go-slow on public transport, which we hope will soon reach an amicable conclusion via negotiation between management and men – (*Murmurings of 'hear, hear' from one or two of the guests*) – to be here with us today. Furthermore, I hope you'll all agree with me, it's been well worth it. (*More 'hear, hears'*) I thought the vicar, God bless him, put on a handsome little service –

POLLY    (*beaming at the world at large*) Beautiful.

DUGGIE    – and we hope you're all have a nice day, one and all. I think apologies are in order re the weather – but that was a technical hitch unfortunately beyond our control – I hope you didn't get too wet with snow . . .

POLLY    (*comfortingly to everyone*) It was quite Christmassy really . . .

DUGGIE    . . . What with the heavens opening up like that –

POLLY    (*to everyone*) It was only the angels throwing confetti. Soon dries.

DUGGIE    . . . And we sincerely hope it hasn't 'dampened' the proceedings!

POLLY    (*battling on*) A few snowflakes, never hurt anyone, did they?

DUGGIE    So . . . er . . . to recap on behalf of Polly and myself . . .

POLLY    Hear, hear.

DUGGIE    . . . Thank you all, and God bless our lovely daughter and her chosen partner in life. I thank you.

*Applause as he sits. Polly leans towards him and whispers.*

POLLY    The toast!

DUGGIE    What?

POLLY    You've to propose to toast to them.

DUGGIE    I just did!

POLLY    You didn't. Not the *toast*.

*Duggie gets to his feet again.*

DUGGIE    So, finally, ladies and gentlemen, I'd like to propose the toast of health and happiness to our lovely daughter and her chosen partner in life and more power to their elbow. I thank you.

*He sits. Corroborative mutterings from the guests. They drink and applaud. Brian stands up.*

BRIAN  (*reading from notes written on the back of the booklet called 'Wedding Etiquette, 50p'*) Thank you, Mr Cook. And now it's my privilege and pleasure to call upon the lucky bridegroom, Warren.

*Warren swivels round to him, in alarm.*

WARREN  (*whispering*) What the hell for???
BRIAN  (*addressing the guests*) To say a few words.
WARREN  (*whispering to Christine*) I thought we'd put our foot down!!
CHRISTINE  (*whispering to Brian*) We said he wasn't going to!!
WARREN  (*whispering back*) Your Mum nobbled me. She said he'd ...
POLLY  (*whispering to Warren*) It's nice, a nice speech. Christine'd appreciate you giving a speech.
CHRISTINE  Me??
POLLY  It's nice.

*To a round of applause, Warren gets to his feet, blowing loudly through his teeth in evident impatience with the whole damn business, and stands in an extremely casual pose.*

WARREN  (*quickly, parrot-like*) I'd like to thank Christine's parents for the wedding, and everyone for coming and for your very useful presents. Ta.

*He promptly sits down again. A slight ripple of shock among the guests at the brevity of his speech and the curtness of his delivery.*

DUGGIE  (*embarrassed*) Short and sweet ...

*A short uncomfortable pause.*

POLLY  (*suddenly trying to laugh it off*) Like me. (*To the guests at large*) Like me, eh? Well, anyway 'and sweet'!

*A little laughter, and a smattering of applause for Warren's speech.*

BRIAN  (*standing again*) Thank you, Warren. Well, now ... um ... (*He checks his notes for what happens next*) ... by popular request, it's now *my* turn. To give a speech. I mean, not get married!

*He laughs at his joke, awkwardly. One or two of the guests laugh politely.*

POLLY  (*to the nearest guests*) It's probably the fashion. Short speeches. I thought Warren's was very nice and to the point. Sincere.

### 6 The kitchen

*Through the door held slightly ajar, Mr Toby is keeping a beady eye on events in the reception room.*

*He closes the door and turns back inside. We hear Brian's muted voice droning on outside.*

MR TOBY  Right! Last speech in progress. Ready with the liqueurs, Carol?

CAROL  (*standing by her drinks trolley*) Ready.

MR TOBY  Coffee organised?

MADGE  Naturally.

MR TOBY  Naturally. (*He calls across to the musicians*) At your convenience, lads. I'll give you the nod! (*The Quartet acknowledge the information and continue drinking their beer*) And you don't take no for an answer with them liqueurs, compre? I only want you back in here with empty bottles.

CAROL  Right.

MR TOBY  And half measures with the coffee, Madge. If they're thirsty, tell them there's plenty of Green Goddess on the trolley.

MADGE  It *is* my 84th wedding, Mr Toby!

MR TOBY  No one said it wasn't.

MADGE  Even Elizabeth Taylor can't say that!

MR TOBY  No one said she could.

### 7 The reception room

*Brian is still on his feet, coming to the end of his speech.*

BRIAN  ... and, in conclusion, a special 'thank you, darling' to our handsome bridesmaids, the lovely Barbara – (*He smiles at Barbara. She smiles politely, and briefly back*) – and Shirley (*He smiles briefly at Shirley. She smiles warmly back*) – who, I'm sure you agree, are looking handsome. (*Hear, hears from the guests, and a beaming smile from Polly to the two bridesmaids*) And, in conclusion, I reckon that's enough from me – specially as I believe the bar is now open! Nudge, nudge, say no more! (*Laughter from the guests*) Now, if all the gentlemen who've had eggs for breakfast would be kind enough to roll their sleeves up, and help out shifting the tables from off of the dance-floor, we will now have dancing to the accompaniment of – (*He reads from his note*) – Harry

Chadwick's radio and TV sensation – The Four Aces in Harmony Quartet! Thank you.

*He sits down to applause.*
*We cut to the feet of the principals beneath the top table. We see that Polly has her shoes off. Her hand comes surreptitiously down into shot, and starts putting them on again.*

## 8 The kitchen

*Mr Toby, peeping through the door, turns and gives the thumbs-up sign to the four lethargic musicians. They stroll to the door, finishing off the pints en route, plonk their empty glasses on a table near the door and exit into the reception room.*

*They're followed by Madge with her coffee pots, and Carol wheeling her trolley of liqueurs.*

## 9 The reception room

*Male guests are lifting the tables from the dance floor, while others grab their coffee cups and half-smoked cigarettes from the tables, before they're snatched away.*

*The musicians make their way through the noisy, disorganised bustle, to their dais, where their instruments are waiting.*

*Polly, Duggie, Christine and Warren are standing to one side waiting for the tables to be organised.*

POLLY   Well, I don't know what's happened to that photographer, I'm sure ...

CHRISTINE   I am.

POLLY   Eh?

CHRISTINE   After that performance outside church.

WARREN   Probably having a fortnight in a flaming funny-farm ...

POLLY   What performance outside church?

WARREN   Well, I've never seen so many pictures of a wedding group!

POLLY   Judging by your speech, Warren, I doubt you've many weddings! (*Pause*) There should be *some* snaps of the head table, and the dancing. As long as he's here when you cut the cake. (*Promptly beaming to a passing guest*) Enjoying yourself, Alice?

ALICE   There was no mayonnaise down our end.

POLLY   (*horrified*) You should've said!

DUGGIE   It's included in the set menu. It's all paid for.

ALICE  Well, there wasn't none. We had to do without.

POLLY  You should've told the waitress!

ALICE  She shouldn't need telling. Not that I ever eat it, myself. Blows me up out here, mayonnaise. (*She continues on her way*)

POLLY  (*to Duggie*) Well . . . they happen don't they, little things? I think it's going a treat, all told. Isn't it Dugg? All told?

DUGGIE  What's old Tom Abbot come in his medals for?

*Polly follows his glance to an elderly man in a well-pressed, threadbare suit sporting a row of medals of the First World War. He is sitting, soldier-like, to attention, at one of the tables.*

POLLY  He means no harm. I don't think he's been out of the house since decimal money came in. I've tried explaining it to him. But he just cries. Isn't it, Christine?

CHRISTINE  What?

POLLY  Going a treat?

*Christine's Uncle Stan and Aunt Dora approach the group, beaming.*

STAN  Now I've one word for her, that's all! 'Delightful'! A vision of delight. You can go through the whole of the Oxford Dictionary – and that's the only one!

DORA  I second that! She looks delightful!

POLLY  (*absolutely thrilled to bits*) Well, thank you, Dora. And you, Stan. I had to take the hem up, mind you. (*She lifts her hem up slightly to show them*) Still . . . God bless Marks and Sparks!

*Stan and Dora look, in puzzlement, from Polly to her hem.*

DORA  Christine . . .

POLLY  Pardon, dear?

DORA  Um . . . *Christine* looks delightful . . . um . . .

POLLY  Oh!

STAN  (*hastily*) Well, *you* as well, Polly. Both of . . . I mean, we didn't mean . . . we meant . . . Well, you all look very, very nice.

CHRISTINE  Thanks, Uncle Stan.

POLLY  (*subdued*) Thank you.

STAN  And how's it feel being a married man, then, Warren?

WARREN  (*bored stiff*) Why? Don't you know?

STAN  (*thrown slightly*) Oh . . . oh yes. Yes, indeed. (*Trying to laugh it off*) The first forty years are the worse, eh, Duggie?

POLLY  (*her spirits bouncing back relentlessly*) And shall we be having the honour of seeing your wing and whisk, I hope?

CHRISTINE  Their what?

POLLY  In the waltz.

DORA  (*smiling regretfully*) Oh, I think my wing and whisk days went out with 'Cruising Down the River'! It really depends if Stan's back's up to it ...

POLLY  (*to Warren*) Stan put his back out for three months.

DUGGIE  (*to Warren*) The day of the Industrial Relations Bill march.

STAN  (*to Warren*) It came out in sympathy!

CHRISTINE  I bet you always say that, don't you, Uncle Stan?

DORA  (*laughing*) Always!

CHRISTINE  I thought so.

*All except Christine and Warren are discomfited by Christine's remark. A moment of awkward embarrassment. Polly promptly tries to gloss it over.*

POLLY  (*to Dora*) Um ... did you have mayonnaise at your end?

STAN  (*baffled by the question*) Er ... did we have ...?

DORA  On the table?

POLLY  Yes.

DORA  Yes.

POLLY  Good.

*They stand, uncomfortable and embarrassed for a few moments longer.*
*Cut to the Quartet tuning up their instruments on the dais; and Carol and Madge dispensing liqueurs and coffee to the guests, who are now reseated at individual tables round the edge of the dance floor.*
*Duggie is watching Carol, puzzled, as Stan and Dora wander off to talk to friends in a group at a table.*

DUGGIE  Liqueurs!! She's lashing out liqueurs.

POLLY  (*following his gaze*) Mmmm. She should have given *us* first, shouldn't she? We *are* top table ...

DUGGIE  She shouldn't be giving anybody!! Liqueurs aren't on the set menu! (*He pulls a menu price list from his jacket pocket and studies it*) 'Set menu D ...' (*muttering his way down it*) ... 'One serving of coffee after meal. Two glasses champagne, Standard Quality De Luxe, per person during speeches.' (*He glances at Madge dispensing coffee*) That's that one. (*Refers back to his list*) No mention whatever of liqueurs. Nowhere. In any shape or form. And do you know why?

POLLY  Why?

DUGGIE  Because it's an extra. It's going to cost us extra!

POLLY  Duggie, it's a wedding!

DUGGIE  I know it's a wedding. The fact hasn't escaped me. It's not likely to at this bloody rate!!!

*Cut to the Quartet's pianist and leader, Harry Chadwick, who is speaking into the microphone.*

CHADWICK  Hello, everyone! Testing, testing, one, two, three, four, fi ... hello , everyone!!! Introducing for your dancing pleasure, straight from our recent triumphant tour – The Four Aces in Harmony!! A-one, a-two, a-one, two, three!

*The Quartet launches into its rendering of 'Congratulations' – as thin and amateurish a sound as is truthfully possible.*
  *Cut back to Polly and Duggie.*

POLLY  (*grabbing Duggie's arm*) Come on!

DUGGIE  Where?

POLLY  It's a quickstep. You can do a quickstep. (*She begins to lead him onto the dance floor, which necessitates squeezing past Brian who's trying to chat up the bridesmaid, Barbara*) 'Scuse me, Brian. (*Barbara immediately realises this is her chance to get away from Brian, and takes it, much to Brian's frustration*) (*Squeezing by*) Very nice speech, by the way. Nice and long.

BRIAN  (*trying to see where Barbara sloped off to*) Ta. Wasn't bad, was it? Where are you off, then?

POLLY  The dancing's started.

BRIAN  (*puzzled*) Well?

POLLY  Well, what?

BRIAN  There's an order of precedence.

POLLY  (*completely baffled*) I know. (*Pause*) An order of what?

BRIAN  Precedence. According to my 'Wedding Etiquette, 50p'. (*He taps his top pocket as proof*) It should be bride and bridegroom first.

DUGGIE  Protocol, I should imagine. They always start the dancing.

POLLY  (*disappointed*) Oh, yes. Yes, I knew that. Of course, they do. (*She calls across to Christine who's standing with Warren*) Christine?

*Christine and Warren look across to her. Polly mimes to them that they should take the floor and start the dancing so that everyone else may dance. Christine and Warren cotton on, hearts sinking at the thought.*

CHRISTINE (*to Warren*) Come on.

WARREN Oh, God . . .

CHRISTINE It's only for a few minutes. Think of West Ham United.

*They make their way to the dance floor and half-heartedly begin dancing. Polly, like a greyhound at the leash, starts dancing with Duggie, loving every second of it.*

*Cut to a table. At the table, sipping their coffee and liqueurs are a young pregnant woman (Denise), her husband (Ronnie) and a middle-aged woman (Poor Auntie Edna). Denise's nine-year-old daughter, Tracy, is playing about nearby with a balloon. Denise and Poor Auntie Edna are watching Christine dancing.*

DENISE It's the same dress as Princess Anne's you know. Different material.

POOR EDNA And without the train, of course.

DENISE And the pearls. She wrote up for it to the Daily Mirror. Well, her mother did. I was half-expecting her turning up in jeans.

POOR EDNA Who's Jean?

DENISE Blue denims. Jeans.

POOR EDNA Oh 'jeans'!! Well . . . young people are like that today.

DENISE Princess Anne wasn't.

POOR EDNA No. *She* had *gorgeous* weather, didn't she?

DENISE Gorgeous.

POOR EDNA Shows you.

*Cut to Polly and Duggie dancing.*

DUGGIE I am not spoiling anything! The price list for Set Menu D was never subject to negotiation or amendment by either party! Extraneous liqueurs at God-knows-how-much a time were not within the frame of reference! It places their entire credibility gap in jeopardy!

POLLY You're supposed to twirl me round now and then.

DUGGIE Eh?

POLLY You keep going in a straight line. It's not a foxtrot. (*He twirls her round. They end up side by side with Christine and Warren, as they dance sulkingly round*) (*Through her fixed, 'public' smile*) Christine?

CHRISTINE What now?

POLLY Stop it.

CHRISTINE Stop what?

POLLY You know what.

*She smiles graciously at other couples as they dance by.*

CHRISTINE  I'm not doing nothing!

POLLY  Aren't you?

DUGGIE  She's alright.

POLLY  Is she?

*Both couples dance apart.*

WARREN  What are you supposed to have done?

CHRISTINE  She's flipped, I'm not kidding. She's getting worse every
minute. Completely bloody flipped. She was beyond belief
this morning. She was only sick, that's all.

WARREN  What – mentally?

CHRISTINE  Vomiting. Vomiting from nerves. And when she wasn't
vomiting, she was bloody weeping. Ten minutes before the
bloody car comes, there I am, in my bridal gown, brewing
her cups of tea and shovelling bloody Librium down her ...

*Cut to Polly and Duggie dancing. Duggie is twisting his head,
this way and that, trying to watch Carol's progress with the
liqueurs.*

DUGGIE  They're going through it like coloured water! Not a soul at
the bar buying their own! Never will while she's at it!

POLLY  Complain to the manager. Not me.

DUGGIE  Don't think I'm not considering it ...

POLLY  *(suddenly scared)* Not *now*, though!

DUGGIE  What?

POLLY  Monday. Complain on Monday.

DUGGIE  Look at her!! She must be giving treble stamps on every
gallon!

POLLY  *(smiling graciously at passing couples)* Duggie, if you say one
more word about liqueurs, I shall drink a bottle of it myself!
And you know you won't complain.

DUGGIE  Who won't?

POLLY  You won't.

DUGGIE  It's not a matter of complaining. It's a matter of principle.

*They're now dancing alongside Warren and Christine again.*

CHRISTINE  *(to Duggie)* Are those liqueurs included in the price?

POLLY  No, they're not!! So your father'll have to do another three
days overtime! Happy now? Now you've something to sulk
about!

CHRISTINE  God, it's stupid! I said all along it was stupid. (*To Duggie*) How much is the whole stupid pantomime costing you?

DUGGIE  Enough.

POLLY  (*very angry*) Now, stop it, both of you! *All* of you! Five months I've had of it! Swearing, arguing, everybody against me! We're here now – and it's lovely – and we're happy – (*Almost in tears*) – very happy – and that's something money can't buy.

*They dance for a moment in silence. Polly tries to control her imminent tears.*

WARREN  Mrs Cook, all I want to –

POLLY  'Mother'.

WARREN  Eh?

POLLY  You're supposed to call me 'Mother' now. I'm only Mrs Cook to the milkman.

WARREN  All I want to know is who's it all for. That's all. (*No reply*) Well? (*No reply*) Us, isn't it? Christine and me? That's the general idea, right?

POLLY  Look, we've *been* through all this! Again and again. Talk about wind up the gramophone!

WARREN  What me and Christine wanted didn't *need* no money to buy! It doesn't *cost* nothing!

POLLY  Living in sin.

CHRISTINE  Living *together*.

POLLY  In sin.

CHRISTINE  *Together.*

POLLY  Together in sin.

CHRISTINE  (*to herself*) Like a bloody brick wall.

WARREN  Alright – even a registry office! A bottle of pale ale and a pork pie at your house ... what more do you need?

POLLY  (*bitterly*) You don't know do you? A grown man. Swanking you're a grown man. And you don't know! (*To Duggie*) Either of you!!

CHRISTINE  Mother, what difference do you think all this'll make to me and Warren? Apart from the grey hairs.

DUGGIE  Look! I am sick up to *here* of listening to this! You've all said it a million times before. You've said nothing *else*. Now, let it drop. Let's move on to any other business. Just let it drop. Once and for all. I thought today meant the argument was over ...

*Both couples dance along in silence for a moment.*

CHRISTINE  (*quietly*) It's hypocrisy. The whole thing. (*Polly ignores her*) It *is* Mum. You've made us *all* hypocrites. I hope you're satisfied.

*Polly smiles sweetly at a couple dancing by.*

POLLY  Alright, Marion?
MARION  Lovely, thank you, Polly. Very nice.
POLLY  Going a treat, isn't it?
MARION  Lovely. (*Pause*) It wasn't tinned, was it?
POLLY  What wasn't?
MARION  The tomato soup.
POLLY  *Cream* of tomato . . . Oh, I don't think so.
MARION  I thought not. That's two and a half p, I've won. You can get tinned at home, can't you. Any day of the week . . .

*They dance by. The music stops, first medley ended. Everyone leaves the floor except Polly. She stands applauding the Quartet, heartily.*
*As she turns to leave the floor, Carol passes wheeling her drinks trolley back towards the kitchens. Polly quickly catches up with her.*

POLLY  May I trouble you, Miss?
CAROL  Certainly, madam.
POLLY  Thank you. (*Carol hands her a liqueur*) Are you warm or is it me?
CAROL  I think they put the heating up once the bar's open. So's people feel dry.
POLLY  Well . . . everyone to his trade. Are you having one yourself?
CAROL  Oh, thank you!
POLLY  Well, special occasion, isn't it? Like when it's Christmas. You can do anything at Christmas. Go for a paddle in Trafalgar Square. Show yourself up. And people just say 'Well, it's Christmas'.
CAROL  I'll have it in the kitchen.
POLLY  Well, it wouldn't be dignified in here, would it? Not really.
CAROL  No. Well, cheers, then.
POLLY  All the best.

*Carol wheels her trolley towards the kitchen. We go with her.*


## 10  The kitchen

*Continuous in time. Queenie is wearily washing up. Mr Toby is adding up figures while sipping from a pint of beer.*
*Carol enters with her trolley.*

| | |
|---|---|
| MR TOBY | (*looking up*) Yes, madam? |
| CAROL | Pardon. |
| MR TOBY | Can I help you? |
| CAROL | I *work* here!! |
| MR TOBY | Exactly. Going round with liqueurs. |
| CAROL | I've *been* round with liqueurs! |
| MR TOBY | Well, go round again! As long as they're swilling coffee, it's perfectly in order to offer liqueuers. (*Carol turns the trolley round, sighing wearily*) Did you speak? |
| CAROL | My leg aches. |
| MR TOBY | My *heart* aches, darling. But somehow I soldier on ... |

*Carol exits with her trolley back into the reception room. Mr Toby settles back contentedly with his beer.*

### 11 The reception room

*Christine and Warren are seated at a table, toying with their coffee.*

*The Quartet is playing yet another passé number (e.g. 'Slow Boat to China'), perhaps with a vocal from Harry Chadwick, half-sung, half-recited like a pub singer.*

*Denise's small daughter, Tracy, is having the time of her life, running and sliding up and down the dance floor near her mother's table.*

| | |
|---|---|
| DENISE | Tracy! Tracy! Come here! (*Tracy ignores her*) Tracy! I shan't tell you again! Come here! (*Tracy ignores her*) Tracy! |

*Tracy, defiantly, continues her sliding.*

| | |
|---|---|
| CHRISTINE | (*to herself*) Good for you Tracy ... |

*A bored pause between Christine and Warren.*

| | |
|---|---|
| WARREN | What do you reckon is a discreet interval? |
| CHRISTINE | Mmm? |
| WARREN | How long do you reckon we have to stay? |
| CHRISTINE | Do you know, I haven't a clue who half these people are ... |
| WARREN | Well, they're all your side. |
| CHRISTINE | God knows where she's dug them up from. See the one with the elastoplast round her glasses. (*She nods towards a woman dancing. Warren follows her gaze*) She isn't even family. Or friend. Or bloody neighbour. She calls once a fortnight with a mail order catalogue. What's she invited *her* for? |

*Suddenly, Denise gets up and drags a protesting, disgruntled Tracy from the dance floor. Tracy resists in vain. Denise pushes her into a chair at their table.*

DENISE    (*sitting*) Now, sit down properly. Like a lady.

*Tracy promptly crawls under the table.*

DENISE    Oh, I'll give you such a good hiding in a minute! (*To Ronnie*) She *won't* let you enjoy yourself. (*She leaps in sudden pain. Tracy, under the table, has apparently banged Denise's foot*) Ow!! Right. I warned you. You're going to no more weddings! Ever. None! And that's final!

CHRISTINE    (*to herself*) Good for you Tracy . . .

*Cut to Polly meandering, like the Queen Mother, from table to table.*

POLLY    Enjoying yourselves, everyone?

1ST GUEST    Yes, thanks Polly. Very nice.

POLLY    Went off well, didn't it?

1ST GUEST    Like clockwork. Lovely.

*She passes to the next table, where an old lady, Mrs Edwards, is having trouble with her hearing aid.*

POLLY    (*shouting*) Alright, Mrs Edwards?

MRS E    (*shouting*) Mick Jagger.

POLLY    (*shouting*) Your hair's nice.

MRS E    (*shouting*) In a bit. They haven't had the Gay Gordons yet, have they?

POLLY    (*shouting*) Not yet.

MRS E    (*shouting*) Not yet.

*Polly passes along to the next table.*

POLLY    Everybody happy? Gladys? Jimmy?

JIMMY    First rate. No question.

GLADYS    A day to remember, Polly.

*Polly seems inordinately touched by the remark. Moved almost to tears.*

POLLY    Thank you Gladys. That's a lovely thing to say. And much and deeply appreciated. Thank you.

GLADYS    Shame his parents couldn't be here. To share the joy.

POLLY    The lucky bridegroom's?

GLADYS    Mmm.

POLLY   Well, he's lost his mum, of course.

GLADYS   Yes.

POLLY   And his dad's unfortunately – you know . . .

GLADYS   Shame.

POLLY   Still, it's definitely a day to remember, isn't it? For *all* of us. (*Carol passes with the drinks trolley*) May I, dear?

CAROL   Certainly, madam.

> *She hands Polly another liqueur.*
>
> *Cut to Duggie at the bar with Uncle Stan. Duggie is calling across to some middle-aged friends who are seated at tables with their wives, sipping liqueurs.*

DUGGIE   Oi, Danny! Harold! Come over here and have one! There's pints going over here, not that muck. Rots your bootlaces. (*A couple of men get up – their wives none too pleased about it – to make their way over to the bar*) That's the idea! (*To Stan*) Sat there like the bloody Monday Club, little fingers stuck in the air. I mean, a pint's something to get your dentures round, isn't it? Something to get hold of. Grown men.

STAN   Same again?

DUGGIE   I'll just have a half.

> *Cut to Harry Chadwick at the microphone.*

CHADWICK   Now then, ladies and gentlemen. Now that you've had a good bashing of the Tops of the Pops –

CHRISTINE   (*incredulously*) When???

CHADWICK   – we'll now get switched on, and really with it, with 'Knees Up, Mother Brown'! And let's have everybody on the floor this time, please! (*To the musicians*) A-one, a-two, a-one, two, three!

> *The Quartet launches into 'Knees up, Mother Brown'. Three or four couples make their way onto the floor. Polly starts making her way back to Christine's table. En route, she passes Dora.*

DORA   Your favourite, Polly. Not dancing?

POLLY   Not this. Well, it's not dignified, really, is it? I mean, for New Year's Eve, yes. VJ night or something.

DORA   You used to love 'Knees Up, Mother Brown'!

POLLY   (*rather grandly*) I used to *do* it, Dora. Yes. Out of sociableness. I didn't *love* it. Not at a wedding. (*She continues on her way, leaving a somewhat puzzled Dora behind. She stops*

*Carol en route, and this time helps herself to another drink*) Thank you dear. (*She sits down at Christine's table, ignoring the hostile vibes from Christine and Warren*) (*To no one in particular*) They should let you pick the songs of your choice. Like in church. What hymns you want.

CHRISTINE  *I* didn't pick no hymns. I wasn't even asked.

POLLY  (*to Warren*) Go on. Your turn.

WARREN  What?

POLLY  You're slipping. You haven't upset me for at least five minutes. Well, you try – and you shan't. Either of you. I've decided.

*Marion, whom we met earlier dancing with her husband, sweeps down on them.*

MARION  Now, I shall entertain no arguments – (*She plonks herself down in a chair*) – and any payment for my services will be considered an insult of the highest order! I feel the power coming on!

POLLY  (*happily, excitedly*) Oh, yes! Yes, Marion! Lovely!

CHRISTINE  You can hardly do our tea-leaves! We've only had coffee!

MARION  I read hands as well as tea-leaves, dear. I was reading hands when platform heels were in fashion the *first* time. Got to see what the future holds haven't we? Today of all days. (*Polly promptly puts her hand out to be read. Marion, expecting Christine's hand, is thrown slightly*) (*To Christine*) Aren't you having yours done, dear?

CHRISTINE  I've a fairly good idea what the future holds, thanks, Marion.

POLLY  (*to Marion*) I'll have mine done, then, shall I? So's you won't have had a wasted journey.

*Marion takes Polly's hand and peruses it. Everything she says is said rapidly, fluently, facilely; she's said precisely the same things to others over a thousand times before.*

MARION  Goodness me, your line of Venus! You do have an affectionate nature, don't you? Do anything for anybody. You worry a lot, don't you, dear? Inside. But you never show it. However much you're suffering. (*To Christine*) It's a wonderful quality, that. (*Resuming her reading*) Now, I see someone in green. And a letter P. Who do you know beginning with P, and this aura of green round them?

POLLY  P? (*Shakes her head*) In green?

MARION   It could be green fields. Or a green dress. A green room, even. Anything green.

WARREN   A billiard table.

MARION   (*slightly offended*) Well, I suppose it *could* be a billiard table. It's not usual. But it's a *man*. Definitely a man.'

POLLY   I can only think of my Auntie Pat. But she *hated* green. She wouldn't give it house-room.

MARION   (*not the subtlest of fortune-tellers*) Or is it a woman? Yes, it is – it's a woman. Definitely. She was probably wearing slacks ... And the green might be something she's trying to avoid, because she doesn't like it ...

POLLY   My Auntie Pat hated it.

MARION   I was right, then. (*She throws Polly's hand aside and studies the other one*) Now, your heart rules your head, doesn't it, dear?

POLLY   I think it sometimes has done ...

MARION   No question. You see, this hand shows what you were born with – and that one what you've achieved. Now, your line of purpose is as straight as an arrow, strong as a die, on the hand you were born with, but –

*She throws the hand aside and takes the other one.*

WARREN   On the other hand ...

MARION   (*after a dirty look*) On the other hand – the events of your life have impeded it. Polly?

POLLY   Yes?

MARION   I think the green is green water ... and there's a bridge ... and she's telling you, Polly, she's telling you to cross the bridge, Polly, to find happiness.

POLLY   Thank you.

MARION   (*glancing at the empty glasses*) Were those liqueurs?

POLLY   Oh, we've all sorts. Cherry brandies, egg flips, Green Goddess ... Didn't you have one?

MARION   I may just have had *one*, I think ...

POLLY   Come on. *I'm* having another.

*She and Marion get up and start after the drinks trolley.*
   *Christine and Warren exchange a wry glance. Christine watches Brian leaving the dance floor with Barbara. She's obviously still not in the least interested in him, and walks off to join other people. Shirley promptly buttonholes Brian, who keeps trying to keep his eye on Barbara, and puts on a big act of being a helpless, hurt little girl ... head lowered, pouting, hoping she's appearing irresistibly heart-melting.*

84

*Christine glances at little Tracy, now sitting between Denise and Ronnie. Tracy is doing precisely the same act as Shirley.*

DENISE And there's no point in looking badly done to! The answer is no! (*Tracy frowns and pouts herself very close to tears, then clambers onto Ronnie's knee*) And don't think you'll get around your daddy, because you won't!

*Christine glances back to Brian and Shirley. Her act is now slightly more seductive ... stroking her finger in little circles on his lapel, stroking his arm, cradling her head against his chest.*

*Christine looks back to Tracy on her Daddy's knee. She's curling a strand of his hair, then his tie, round and round in her fingers.*

TRACY Go on, Daddy! Please.
DENISE No.
TRACY Please, Daddy, dance with me.
RONNIE Tracy! Behave!
TRACY Nice, daddy. Bestest daddy. Please, daddy!
RONNIE (*sighing*) Just this once.

*Tracy immediately stops her act and jumps down excitedly to drag Ronnie to the dance floor.*

*Christine looks back to Brian and Shirley. She's whispering in his ear, still little-girlishly. He nods. She at once relinquishes her act, and leads Brian, by the hand, to a door marked 'PRIVATE KEEP OUT'. They go in.*

*Cut to Polly, now slightly tipsy, approaching the musicians' dais, glass in hand. She taps Harry Chadwick on the leg.*

POLLY Excuse me, Geraldo.
CHADWICK (*amused*) Do me a favour!
POLLY Can you play 'Ramona'?
CHADWICK On my head, sweetheart.
POLLY And 'Oh, how we danced on the night we were wed'?
CHADWICK Certainly, darling.
POLLY Thank you. (*She starts to move away*)
CHADWICK See you later, mashed potato!
POLLY (*absolutely naturally, automatically, as a reflex*) In an hour, cauliflower.

*She wanders off. Harry Chadwick – very, very puzzled – stares after her.*

DRUMMER What's up?
CHADWICK Hear that?

DRUMMER  What?

CHADWICK  By hell, that took me back!

DRUMMER  What did she say?

CHADWICK  (*deeply thoughtful*) Now, where do I know her from? Where've I met *that* one before . . . ?

*Cut to Polly, crossing the edge of the dance floor, near to the door to the foyer. Christine is standing there, watching the dancing.*

POLLY  (*sarcastically*) It's being so cheerful as keeps you going, isn't it?

CHRISTINE  Sorry, I didn't recognise you for the minute. Till I saw the glass in your hand.

POLLY  You're spoiling it all, you know that, don't you? Giving your dirty looks . . .

CHRISTINE  Look, Mum. We've done what you wanted. Right. Just don't expect me to *enjoy* it into the bargain!

POLLY  *I'm* enjoying it.

CHRISTINE  I'll say! Mother, it's not a game! No, hang about, that's *exactly* what it is! I feel sick.

POLLY  (*suddenly apprehensive*) What do you mean – you feel sick?

CHRISTINE  You know what I mean.

POLLY  (*hopefully*) It'll be the heat . . . the excitement . . .

CHRISTINE  You *know* what it'll be. The whole bloody reason we're here!

*Polly smacks Christine's face – just as the music comes to an end, so that the smack is audible to everyone. Everyone looks. Christine dashes into the foyer, followed by Polly.*

## 12  The foyer

*Christine dashes in from the reception room and through a door marked 'LADIES'. Polly follows and stands outside. Warren enters from the reception room.*

WARREN  What happened? Who hit who? Which one of you . . . ? (*He notices that Polly is quietly weeping*) Look, she's a bit strung up. We all are. It's only natural.

POLLY  She should be having the time of her life.

WARREN  She'll be alright once today's over with.

POLLY  It must *never* be over with. It's here for ever. That's the whole point! It's *never* forgotten.

## 13 The reception room

*The band is playing. Harry Chadwick, still deep in thought, keeps glancing through the open doors to Polly in the foyer ... Trying to remember ...*

## 14 The reception room

*An hour or so later. The Quartet is playing 'It's a Wonderful World'; perhaps with a vocal from Harry Chadwick.*

*Polly, now even tipsier, is dancing with Duggie, desperately throwing herself, heart and soul, into enjoying the occasion. During the song, pan round the guests, who – in sharp contrast to Polly – now seem a bit weary, their hairdos and finery a little dishevelled, yawning, perhaps one or two arguing, and one or two beginning to nod off.*

## 15 The kitchens

*During the song, mutedly audible from the Reception Room, we now see the elderly Queenie, achey and arthritic, hard at work, washing a pile of dishes; while Mr Toby, feet up on a trestle table, sips his beer.*

## 16 The reception room

*The Quartet is still playing 'It's a Wonderful World' over the following tableaux:*

*Brian and Shirley are seen emerging, somewhat sheepishly from the door marked 'PRIVATE KEEP OUT', while surreptitiously rearranging their slightly dishevelled clothing. Once out, they separate and go off in different directions – probably for ever. Barbara sees them come out, cottons on to what's happened, and begins to look at Brian with a new interest.*

*Marion is reading Dora's hand. As she presses it back to read the lines, Dona yelps in pain, pulls it away and rubs it.*

*Tom Abbot, resplendent in his medals, notices that his smart, military appearance is spoilt by the fact that his fly buttons are undone. He buttons them up, hoping he's not being noticed.*

*Tracy, standing beside Denise, is now doing her maternal act – waving a severely-authoritative finger at the as yet unborn baby.*

TRACY    Now just be a good girl! No, you cannot dance with your mummy! Behave yourself or I shall smack you! Naughty, horrid, naughty girl!

*Christine, holding hands with Warren at their table, watches Tracy's adoption of adulthood in dismay. She feels Tracy has let her down.*

CHRISTINE    (*to herself*) Oh, no . . .!
WARREN    What?
CHRISTINE    Nothing.

*Suddenly, Mr Lee, a middle-aged neighbour of Polly's bears heartily down on them.*

MR LEE    So this is where you're hiding!
CHRISTINE    (*sighing on seeing him*) Oh, hello, Mr Lee.

*He promptly sits down.*

WARREN    (*to himself*) Jesus . . .
MR LEE    (*to Warren*) Well, now, Trevor . . .
CHRISTINE    Warren.
MR LEE    Eh?
CHRISTINE    Trevor was eighteen months ago. Trevor was the car-wash mechanic. Warren's a plumber. (*To Warren*) Mr Lee lives next door to the off-licence. The house with 'Marples Must Go' painted on the wall.
WARREN    Who's Marples?
MR LEE    Well, now, Warren. And how's married life treating you? Or is it too early to tell? (*Nudges him and laughs*) Eh? (*Nudges him again*) Tell me better tomorrow morning, eh? (*Winks, then turns to Christine*) He'll tell me better tomorrow morning, dirty devil! (*He gets up again, laughing*) Anyway, see you at the bar, Warren. (*Nudges him*) Got one or two good un's for you.

*He goes off laughing. Christine and Warren watch him go soberly.*

WARREN    When I was in church, waiting for you, I worked out this great system to stop myself going bananas. So's I wouldn't wrap the stained glass window round your mother's neck. All I did was go through the West Ham team in my head. Just sort of listing the players' names. Starting with the goalie right through to number eleven. (*Pause*) And now I can't think of *one* of them . . .

CHRISTINE  *I* feel a bit better now.

WARREN  Not sick?

CHRISTINE  Not anything really. Just sort of numb, I like it.

WARREN  Well, the worst is over now.

CHRISTINE  (*smiling*) Just got the *rest* of our married life to stagger through, that's all.

WARREN  Hey, Chrissie.

CHRISTINE  What?

WARREN  What did you mean earlier on?

CHRISTINE  When?

WARREN  Telling what'shername – (*Nodding towards Marion*) – Gipsy Petrulengo over there – you knew what the future holds?

CHRISTINE  Well, we do, don't we?

WARREN  Do we?

CHRISTINE  Roughly. Yeah. I can see exactly the sort of places we'll live in. The furniture. Wallpaper. I think I even know what we'll be having for tea every day.

WARREN  You never know – might win the pools . . .

CHRISTINE  Oh, you'll sit *doing* them every week. But we won't win. (*Pause*) Then we'll have kids. Kicking holes out the three-piece suite, and crying when you pull the sticking-plasters off, and pinching things from Woolworth's, and giving us cheek. And you'll start getting a pot on you, and fixing yourself up with a bit of spare on the side now and then. And I'll no doubt dye my hair, and watch the wrestling on telly a lot. We'll be like my mum and dad.

WARREN  Great.

CHRISTINE  (*laughs*) Not to worry. You said the worst was over. At least for today. She's said her piece now. She won't open her mouth again.

*Immediately we cut to the band striking up 'Oh, how we danced on the night we were wed', with Polly on the dais, singing the vocal into the microphone, with every ounce of feeling she's got. This is a moment Polly regards as of the utmost importance in her life. She's singing about herself.*

*Cut back to Christine and Warren, horrified.*

CHRISTINE  Oh, my God!

WARREN  You don't think she's coming on the honeymoon as well, do you?

CHRISTINE Come on! (*She stands up and calls across to Brian who's now chatting up Barbara*) Brian! Brian! (*He turns*) Got a minute?

*Cut to Polly,, singing her heart out. Brian joins Christine and Warren.*

BRIAN What have I forgotten?

CHRISTINE Can you run us back to my Mum's. I've got to get changed.

BRIAN Now?

*He looks at his watch.*

CHRISTINE Now.

BRIAN It's not supposed to finish till half-five.

CHRISTINE Not for me, lover. It finished the second that started. (*To Warren*) OK?

WARREN (*getting up*) Right on.

*The three of them make their way purposefully across the dance floor towards the foyer.*

*Polly see them. At first she's puzzled, then realises what's happening. A moment of concern and indecision as to whether she should climb down and stop them.*

*Harry Chadwick watches her carefully. She continues singing her song ... but is now agitated.*


## 17 The foyer

*Christine is standing alone, waiting. We hear Polly's song come to an end, followed by a little applause. Brian and Warren emerge from the men's cloakroom, struggling into their raincoats. Polly hurries in from the reception room.*

POLLY What's going on?

CHRISTINE Nothing.

POLLY (*distressed*) You can't go yet. The hall's booked till 5.30, unless owing to unforeseen circumstances ...

WARREN Well, that's what *this* is.

POLLY What?

CHRISTINE I'm only going to get changed!

POLLY It's too early.

WARREN The traffic may be bad, Mrs Cook.

POLLY I said you could call me Mother.

WARREN It's always bad to Brighton.

POLLY You're going on the train.

WARREN   Yeah. That's what I meant. I meant, you know, if the train was packed ...

*There's a sad little pause. Polly is upset and Christine – now that it's come to it – feels sorry for her, sorry and guilty.*

POLLY   (*quietly*) Everyone will think it's going-home time if *you* go ... (*She catches sight of Poor Auntie Edna coming out of the 'Ladies'*) You didn't meet Poor Auntie Edna, did you, Warren.

CHRISTINE   Look, Mum, we ...

POLLY   (*calling*) Edna!

CHRISTINE   He can meet poor Auntie Edna another time!

*Poor Auntie Edna hobbles over, to them.*

POLLY   You didn't meet Christine's Warren, did you?

POOR EDNA   No.

POLLY   This is Warren.

POOR EDNA   Yes, very nice.

POLLY   (*to Warren*) This is Poor Auntie Edna.

WARREN   Hi.

*They all stand awkwardly for a moment.*

POOR EDNA   Very nice.

*She goes off back into the reception room.*

CHRISTINE   Mother, we'll call back in to say ta-ta!

POLLY   You haven't even cut the cake yet. (*To Warren*) You like marzipan.

CHRISTINE   (*sighing impatiently – because of her guilt and despite her sympathy*) We'll cut it when we call back to say ta-ta!!

BRIAN   Well, come on then, if you're coming!

*They start to go. Polly stands.*

POLLY   Christine? (*Christine turns*) It's only once in a lifetime. You won't regret it when you're older. Look back on it. On the photos. You'll have memories.

CHRISTINE   See you in a bit, Mum.

*Christine, Warren and Brian exit.*

## 18 The reception room

*The Quartet are arranging their music, ready for the next appalling medley.*

CHADWICK  (*to the drummer*) I had this routine, you see. Oh I'm going back a bit now . . . Trio, I had. Did the odd knees-up. Pubs and so forth, nothing special. Made a bob or two. Anyway, I had this corny routine . . . well, it sounds corny now. Went down a bomb in them days. Little comedy number – everyone joined in – sort of audience-participation, really. 'See you later, alligator' –

DRUMMER  'In a while, crocodile.' Handsome.

CHADWICK  Right. Only *we* had 'See you later, mashed potato!, In an hour, cauliflower!', then, next verse, 'See you later, squashed tomato!, In a week, bubble and squeak', then, next verse –

DRUMMER  I think I can get the idea, thanks.

CHADWICK  'See you later, call the waiter, Mind the pips, fish and chips'.

DRUMMER  Jesus . . .

CHADWICK  Different sense of humour today, of course.

DRUMMER  Right.

CHADWICK  Now, where she heard me performing, I don't know. I only did the odd – (*He stops abruptly*) That's it! That's bloody it, isn't it! She sang *then* as well!

DRUMMER  Not like she did here, I hope . . .

CHADWICK  (*trying to remember*) I just can't think what she – It wasn't 'Knees Up, Mother Brown' . . . Could've been 'I've got a lovely ·bunch of coconuts'! Something like that . . . something highly classical . . .

## 19 Polly's living room

*Open on the framed photograph on the sideboard. It's a half-length photo of Duggie and Polly some twenty years ago. Duggie is in the uniform of a merchant seaman and they both have flowers in their lapels. Behind them is a wall of a building bearing a plaque reading 'Newcastle Register Office'.*

*Warren is flopped in an easy chair, reading the half-time football match results in The Evening Standard stop-press. Brian is stacking a couple of suitcases onto the table.*

BRIAN  How are they getting on? Don't tell me.

WARREN  Drawing no-score. 'S'alright, they'll pop one in in the second half.

BRIAN  Who? Us or Everton?

WARREN  Do me a favour. I've had enough lumber for one day. (*Pause*) How did you make out with Shirley, then?

BRIAN  (*with unconvincing innocence*) Shirley?

WARREN  There was a score there alright, wasn't there?

BRIAN  Was there?

WARREN  *I* saw you sloping off. Naughty. I thought it was Barbara you fancied?

BRIAN  It was. She didn't want to play.

*Christine enters from upstairs, now changed into her normal clothes and carrying another small suitcase.*

WARREN  Fit?

CHRISTINE  Can you just do my back up? (*She turns for him to zip up the back of her dress. He's still reading the paper*) Warren!

WARREN  Alright!

CHRISTINE  You used to like doing my back up!

WARREN  I'm doing it! I'm doing it!

*He gets up to attend to the zip.*

CHRISTINE  Alright for money, are we? (*Warren taps his breast pocket to indicate he has money in his wallet*) Right, then.

WARREN  Not forgotten anything?

CHRISTINE  Well, if I said yes, that'd show I'd remembered, wouldn't it?

WARREN  (*surprised at her sharp tone*) Alright! Alright! Don't take it out on me!

CHRISTINE  (*even more niggly*) Take what out on you??

BRIAN  Oi!! (*They both look at him*) Five minutes you've been married? Alright? Now, then, what's the agenda? Bang, bang and back to the dance, quick ta-ta to everyone, then Victoria Station, right?

WARREN  Right.

CHRISTINE  Going to be dead early for the 16.40, aren't we?

WARREN  So we'll catch an earlier one, big deal.

CHRISTINE  What if there isn't an earlier one?

WARREN  We'll sit in the waiting room and play I-bloody-Spy! It was your idea, wasn't it!!

CHRISTINE  I know. I know.

*Warren and Brian take the cases and start making their way to the door. Christine stands where she it, looking round the room, soberly.*

WARREN  (*stopping*) Now what?

CHRISTINE  Warren, I have lived here all my life! I just wanted to look at it a minute.

WARREN  And as long as I've known you, you couldn't get out of it quick enough.

*She starts towards the door. Brian has now exited into the hall and out to the car.*

    *Christine stops by the sideboard and looks at the photo of Duggie and Polly. She picks it up.*

CHRISTINE  It can't all have been because of this, can it?

WARREN  (*stopping again*) All what? Because of what?

CHRISTINE  Just because she was only married at a Registry Office. Giving me something *she* never had ... Newcastle, it was. Because my dad only had a couple of hours ashore. And no relatives there, no friends, no family. And I wasn't even thought of ...

WARREN  Christine, my bloody arm's dropping off.

CHRISTINE  You know that dress she's wearing today? It cost more than my wedding dress.

*Warren watches her troubled. Slightly scared of her mood. We hear Brian hoot the car horn outside a couple of times.*

CHRISTINE  You know that woman, Marion? I know she can't read hands. Takes her all her time to read the *News of the World*. But you know what *I* thought? Someone beginning with P. In green. Helping my mother to happiness. I thought that P was *herself*. P for Polly. But I couldn't think what the green stood for. Only envy.

*Brian hoots the horn again.*

WARREN  Oi! Daydream!

CHRISTINE  Right.

*They both exit.*

## 20 The reception room

*The band is playing something bright and brassy in immediate contrast to the mood of the last scene.*

*Polly has buttonholed the photographer at the bar. He's indicating with his head different groups of guests.*

P/GRAPHER  Yes, Yes. I've done *them*. And *them*. Yes, and the –

POLLY  Have you done the lady in the mauve? Only she's had a slipped disc – and I promised her faithfully . . .

P/GRAPHER  I've done them *all*, Mrs Cook. *And* I'll do the cake-cutting and the bride and groom leaving. It's all under control, missus.

POLLY  And what about the write-up?

P/GRAPHER  What write-up?

POLLY  In the *Kentish Town Gazette* and the *Camden News* and –

P/GRAPHER  Didn't you fill a form in saying bride's name and where she works and the colour of the bridesmaids' dresses and the church and everything?

POLLY  Well, that's just a form, isn't it? It's not a proper write-up. There should be a real reporter here by rights. *They* make something out of nothing.

P/GRAPHER  I just take the photos, missus. I send one of the bride and groom –

POLLY  What about the wedding group?

P/GRAPHER  Yeah . . . . or the wedding group –

POLLY  I mean it's a proper record when it's in the paper. There's plenty about wars and fighting and trouble. It's something to cut out and show people . . .

*There's a hubbub in the foyer. Polly turns to look. Christine and Warren, with Brian to one side, their coats over their arms, are at the door calling goodbye to everyone. Mutters from the guests of 'Oh, they're going!', 'Not going yet, are you?'*

POLLY  (*to herself*) Oh, no . . . Not already . . .

*The guests start their way to Christine and Warren at the door.*

## 21 The foyer

*Warren and Christine are hurriedly taking their leave of well-wishers (pottering through from the reception room) and very anxious to be on their way.*

*Much shaking of hands and slaps on the back, and remarks like
'Now, don't do anything I wouldn't do' – promptly followed by 'That
doesn't leave much, does it?!' and 'If you can't be good, be careful',
'Have an early night', 'Don't do anything you can't do on a bicycle'.
Polly makes her way through the mob, reassurring everyone.*

POLLY    They're having to leave early owing to arrange-
ments ... We're going on for ages yet ... We've got a firm
booking ... We're still having dancing ...

*Duggie ploughs his way through to Christine and Warren. He shakes
Warren's hand.*

DUGGIE    All the best, then, son.
WARREN    Thanks, Mr Cook.

*Duggie turns to Christine. A small moment between them.*

DUGGIE    See you then, Sparrer-legs.
CHRISTINE    (*touched: grins*) See you, Dad. And thanks.
DUGGIE    What the hell for?
CHRISTINE    (*touched*) I can't think.

*Polly has struggled through to join them.*

DUGGIE    (*to Christine*) Wasn't as bad as you thought, was it?
CHRISTINE    It was smashing.

*She and Polly give each other a tiny smile.
    Warren is a little thrown by Christine's attitude, which he feels
has been changing ever since they left the reception earlier.*

POLLY    You looked a picture in your dress.
CHRISTINE    So did you.
POLLY    No one noticed where I pinned your arm-hole up.
BRIAN    (*calling from the door*) I'm parked at a bus-stop.
WARREN    With you, Squire!
BRIAN    There's nowhere else to park ...

*Christine and Warren make their way to the front door. Cries of good
luck from the guests.*

SHIRLEY    Christine! Your bouquet! You're supposed to chuck your
bouquet!

*Christine – laughing like a conventional bride is expected to do (and
again puzzling Warren) – throws the bouquet into the crowd.*

*Shirley tries to catch it – and drops it. Polly picks it up, holds it for a moment, looking at it, then hands it back to Shirley.*

*Christine, Warren and Brian exit amid shouts from everyone.*

*The camera stays on Polly soberly watching Shirley with the bouquet.*

## 22 The kitchen

*We hear the band playing in the reception room. Carol, Madge and Queenie are clearing crockery and glasses away. Queenie then starts on the next pile of washing up. Mr Toby is checking how many liqueurs have been drunk from the trolley, and noting figures on a list.*

MADGE  *(to Mr Toby)* Your Majesty? *(He ignores her)* Your Royal Highness? *(He ignores her)* Mr Toby?

MR TOBY  Yes, Madge?

MADGE  What about the pots of tea and sandwich spread sandwiches?

MR TOBY  What *about* the pots of tea and sandwich spread sandwiches?

MADGE  Well, aren't we doing them?

MR TOBY  Afternoon tea is optional on request. 'On request' being the operative phrase and consequently printed in italics. And thus far it has not been requested.

MADGE  So we don't do them, then?

MR TOBY  I've just explained, haven't I?

CAROL  Well, what do we do now, then? Have a rest?

MR TOBY  'Have a rest'? You've done nothing but rest since you clocked on! It's a wonder your muscles haven't seized up. Look, it'll all be over in twenty minutes. It always shudders to a halt once the happy couple have sodded off into the sunset. Then we clear away, tidy up, and bob's your uncle. Then you can go home and have all the rest you want.

QUEENIE  *(to no one in particular)* *I* can't. I'll have the washing-up to do there as well . . .

## 23 The reception room

*A little later. The band is playing a slow, sleepy number – matching exactly the mood of the guests. Tracy is now fast asleep on Ronnie's knee. Old Tom Abbot, still sitting to attention is also fast asleep. One or two guests are stretching wearily, yawning, glancing at watches. Polly is sitting alone at a table. Duggie comes up from the bar, carrying a glass of fizzing water.*

DUGGIE   Here you are, girl. Try that for size.

POLLY   What is it?

DUGGIE   Never mind what it is. The barman says it'll make you better.

POLLY   Shouldn't I have black coffee?

DUGGIE   You can have black coffee at home. It's cheaper.

POLLY   We haven't got no coffee.

DUGGIE   I'm talking about the principle, not the shop-floor ramifications! Drink up.

*Polly does so and pulls a face.*

POLLY   It'll never beat liqueurs!

*Gladys and Jimmy pass the table.*

GLADYS   Well, thank you very much, Polly. And you, Duggie.

POLLY   Gladys – you're not going!

GLADYS   Well, we wouldn't if it was up to us, dear, you know that. His mum bangs the telly a lot if it's wonky while we're out. It's been lovely, though, it really has.

POLLY   Nice, wasn't it?

GLADYS   Lovely.

JIMMY   Take care, then, Duggie.

DUGGIE   See you, Jimmy, boy.

*Cut to the Quartet, playing. Harry Chadwick is watching Gladys and Jimmy going.*

CHADWICK   Coming up to happiness-time, lads! The first ones've started. (*To the drummer suddenly*) 'Polly'! That's it! Her name's Polly! That's what she sang – 'Polly put the kettle on!'

*The drummer stares at him, po-faced.*

DRUMMER   You had some wild times, them days, didn't you? What did you do for an encore? Comb your bloody hair?

CHADWICK   'Course, she was three sheets to the wind, at the time.

DRUMMER   I'm glad she had *something* in her favour! (*Harry Chadwick gets up from the piano*) Going to bed?

CHADWICK   Carry on without me for a minute.

DRUMMER   We always *do*, mate!

CHADWICK   You're telling me.

*He climbs down from the dias.*

DRUMMER   Sounds better without you.
CHADWICK   Why? Who's listening?

*More guests are now around Polly, making their excuses to leave. Polly, now standing up, is too tired and drained to plead overmuch.*

DORA   (*to Polly*) Only we did promise our Debbie and Gordon we'd babysit for them. She hasn't been out for six months. She's had a new coat for five. And she's only worn it in the house. When the power cuts were on.
POLLY   Just five minutes, Dora.
STAN   We've got to get to Putney, you see. That's the fly in the ointment.
POLLY   I mean, officially we're booked till 5.30. Six o'clock if it's fine, but 5.30 if it's wet, so's they can mop round the foyer a bit, before the next function.
DORA   Shame.
STAN   Never mind.
DORA   Bye, bye, then, dear. And thank you very much for a lovely time.
STAN   I second that.

*They start to disengage.*

POLLY   Thank *you*. I second that.

*Stan and Dora move off towards the door. Harry Chadwick approaches Polly.*

CHADWICK   Excuse me.

*Polly turns.*

POLLY   Oh, I couldn't sing again! My throat's like sandpaper!
CHADWICK   Eh? Oh, no . . . no, listen. Is your name Polly, or am I wrong?
POLLY   (*smiling*) No, you're right!
CHADWICK   I thought so! Bet you don't remember me, do you?

*Polly studies his face . . . at a loss.*

POLLY   Um . . . I don't quite . . .
CHADWICK   Harry Chadwick.
POLLY   (*it means nothing to her*) Oh, yes?

CHADWICK If I were to say Newcastle Registry Office, nineteen-fifty-something ...

POLLY (*brightly*) Oh, yes?

CHADWICK The little pub round the corner – at the reception ...

POLLY (*face falling; frightened*) Were you there?

CHADWICK Yes.

POLLY In person?

CHADWICK The very day you were ...

POLLY (*interrupting brusquely*) I've never been to Newcastle. You're mistaking me for some other Polly ... some other woman ... my name's not Polly. Excuse me.

*She goes off to bid goodbye to other guests. Harry Chadwick stares after her, blankly.*

### 24 The kitchen

*Mr Toby is peering through the door, waiting for the last guests to leave. Carol and Madge stand at the ready, with their dust-pans, handbrushes and brooms. Queenie is putting her coat on.*

QUEENIE I can do the ashtrays with my coat on. The ashtrays won't mind.

CAROL Ready yet, Mr Toby?

MR TOBY Hang on.

*He gives a thumbs-up sign through the doorway.*

### 25 The reception room

*Harry Chadwick has now made his way back to his piano, and is about to rejoin the Quartet in the middle of the number they're playing.*

*He glances towards the kitchen door and see Mr Toby's signal, and gives him a thumbs-up in reply.*

*He then gives a nod to the drummer, who at once plays a rapid drum-roll bringing the number to a very sudden and premature end.*

*The Quartet then immediately launches into 'God save the Queen'.*

*Polly, at the foyer door, bidding farewell to people, turns on hearing the anthem.*

POLLY They didn't play the last waltz ... I was looking forward to the last waltz ...

*She and Duggie continue their goodbyes to the last stragglers. Denise and Ronnie (with Tracy fast asleep over Ronnie's shoulder) say their thanks and goodbyes and exit. Old Tom Abbot stands in the middle of the dance floor, saluting the band, while the National Anthem is played. Harry Chadwick increases the tempo – rushing it through faster and faster to an abrupt end. Old Tom Abbot makes his slow erect way out. Immediately the Anthem is over, the musicians start to ram their instruments hurriedly into their cases.*

*Immediate cut to:*

## 26 The kitchen

*Mr Toby, at the door, at once turns to Carol and Madge.*

MR TOBY    That's it! Action stations. Ashtrays and crockery first, tablecloths shaken and folded, tables and chairs stacked away – then the place swept out like it's all never happened in the memory of man.

*Carol exits. Madge stops on her way through the door.*

MADGE    (*sympathetically*1) I bet you must be tired out of an evening, Mr Toby.

MR TOBY    (*suspiciously*) Why?

MADGE    Non-stop, isn't it? All go.

MR TOBY    (*martyredly*) Pretty tired . . . yes.

MADGE    All that opening and closing your mouth. And not a bloody word worth saying ever coming out . . .

*She exits.*

## 27 The reception room

*Harry Chadwick is making his way towards the kitchen. The other musicians, carrying their instrument cases, make their way to the foyer.*
   *Carol and Madge start clearing up.*
   *Polly and Duggie are left.*

DUGGIE    Well, that's it, then.

POLLY    Looks like it.

DUGGIE    No further business.

POLLY    No.

DUGGIE I'll ... er ... I'll go and get the mini.

*He starts to go.*

POLLY They all enjoyed it, Duggie.

DUGGIE Oh, yes. Unanimous.

POLLY Did *you*?

DUGGIE Me?

POLLY Yes.

DUGGIE Well ... yes. Of course I did.

POLLY That's the main thing.

DUGGIE Won't be a tick.

*He exits into the foyer.*
    *Polly wanders over to the dais and sits on the edge, sadly watching Carol and Madge clearing up the wreckage. Carol, as she works, is humming to herself 'Oh, how we danced on the night we were wed'.*
    *Polly watches her, a little tearfully. Then – halfway through –*

POLLY (*calling to Carol*) Miss? Miss?

CAROL Yes, madam?

POLLY Can I help you?

CAROL Help me?

POLLY Clearing up.

CAROL (*confused*) Um ... well, I mean you're the ... I don't think you're suppo –

POLLY (*getting up*) I'll give you a hand with the tablecloths. It's easier for two.

*She goes over to her. They start folding a tablecloth.*
    *Harry Chadwick enters from the kitchen. Polly turns her back to avoid him. He continues through to the foyer.*
    *Sudden Carol notices the wedding cake on the top table.*

CAROL The cake!!

POLLY What?

CAROL She never cut the wedding cake!!

*They both look, for a long moment, at the cake.*

POLLY Oh, dear.

CAROL Blimey!

POLLY Would you credit it? (*Pause*) Too late now.

CAROL Yes.

POLLY They'll be half way to – (*Suddenly*) Do you want a piece?

CAROL     (*Smiles*) Go on, you can have a wish!

CAROL     But it's the bride, isn't it? It's the bride that's supposed –

POLLY     'S'alright. I'll do it. You get me a knife, eh?

*She wipes her hands on her sides, and starts towards the table.*

## 28  The foyer

*The Quartet are at the front door, now, wearing their coats.*

*Harry Chadwick, his coat over his arm, is distributing pound notes to them in turn.*

*Duggie enters from the street, and starts towards the men's cloakroom.*

*Harry Chadwick steps away from the others and approaches Duggie.*

CHADWICK     Excuse me, gov'nor.

DUGGIE     Yes, Squire?

CHADWICK     We've met before. (*Duggie looks at him puzzled*) You and the missus.

DUGGIE     (*suddenly wary*) 'Missus'? (*Then brightening*) Oh, Polly, you mean?

CHADWICK     Nineteen-fifty-something. Newcastle. Me and my trio played in the boozer after your mate's wedding. A sailor with a beard. Right? And you were wearing your sailor-suit and she sang 'Polly put the kettle on'! How am I doing?

*Duggie has been listening uncomfortably and a little scared to what had always been his and Polly's secret.*

DUGGIE     Yeah ... that was us ...

CHADWICK     And there were lots of mickey-taking going on about how wasn't it time you and Polly got married ... what with her being in the family way ...

DUGGIE     (*uncomfortably*) Yeah ... well, all in fun.

CHADWICK     It was her I really remembered. Driving you crackers to have a picture taken outside the Registry Office for a lark. You were best man, and she was bridesmaid, right?

DUGGIE     (*guiltily*) Well, *witnesses*, we were ... That's what they call you ...

CHADWICK     Great wedding your mate's was.

DUGGIE     Yes.

CHADWICK     Don't make them like that any more.

DUGGIE  No, well . . . nice to have bumped into you again.

*He starts off into the men's cloakroom.*

CHADWICK  All the best.

### 29  The reception room

*Polly is cutting the wedding cake.*

POLLY  There you are, dear (*She gives Carol a slice*) And one for you. (*She takes a bite from the first piece*) Mmmmm! I could really make a fool of myself over marzipan! Made a wish?

CAROL  Yes. Sort of. Have you?

POLLY  Me? (*Pause*) Oh, a long time ago . . . (*Carol looks at her, not understanding: Polly briskly brightens up*) Come on, then – tablecloths! (*She places the wedding cake on a chair; they go opposite ends of the table and start folding the cloth*) All over now. All the arguments, and the shouting and the . . . Everyone said it was a lovely wedding . . .

CAROL  Beautiful.

POLLY  A white wedding . . . Church . . . everything. Respectable married woman now . . . No one can take that away. Photos and a write-up and dancing . . . and singing . . . well, it's all happy memories, isn't it? (*Pause*) There's a lot of young people today don't know what respectable *means* even. No sense of values. I mean people respect you if you're respectable, don't they? Gives you a bit of dignity . . .

DUGGIE  (*out of view*) Oi! Missus! (*Cut to Duggie at the foyer door now wearing his coat, and carrying Polly's coat over his arm*) Come on, I'm parked at the bus stop!

POLLY  Righto, dear.

*She picks up the cake.*

DUGGIE  And half the bloody wedding guests are queuing, waiting for a bus. I feel uncomfortable.

POLLY  I'm coming, I'm coming.

DUGGIE  Who's the one with the hearing-aid? Mrs Edwards? She keeps asking me for a lift. At the top of her bloody voice.

*He turns to go.*

POLLY  Well, wait for me! We'll walk out *together*, Duggie!

DUGGIE  No, I'll get back to the car before someone nicks the *other* wing mirror . . .

*He exits.*

*Polly carrying the cake, starts across the dance floor. For a moment, she fingers her wedding ring as she walks. Madge and Carol are sweeping and tidying up.*

*Emotionally exhausted, and looking a small, tired, and very lonely figure, Polly makes her way across the deserted dance floor towards the foyer. Halfway across, she takes off a shoe that's hurting her, and limps the rest of the way to the door, and out.*

# Well, Thank You, Thursday

## The Cast

Miss Shepherd, *late 30s or early 40s*
Barry, *mid-30s*
Glenda, *late 20s*
Stan, *early 20s*
Liz, *early 20s*
Mr Crabtree, *80-ish*
Jenny, *19*
Dr Benson
Dan, *in his 60s*
First mother
Second mother
Old man in post office
Mr Patel
Woman shopper
Window cleaner
Mick, *early 20s*
Mary, *early 20s*
First man in overalls
Second man in overalls
Registrar
Extras in post office

# Well, Thank You, Thursday

## 1 Barry's and Glenda's bedroom

*The bedroom is half-lit by morning light through chinks in the curtains. Barry and Glenda are asleep in bed. At the other side of the room we can discern the shape of a baby's crib – and various baby's accoutrements dotted around.*

*Suddenly the peace is disturbed by the baby waking and beginning to cry. Barry and Glenda immediately, reflexively begin to stir in their bed.*

BARRY   (*eyes closed: still almost totally unconscious*) Glenda. Seed o'clock fix.

*Glenda grunts weakly from the depths of sleep.*

BARRY   Seed o'clock fix, Glenda. (*He slowly opens his eyes: puzzled at what his sleepy-slack mouth has just said*) Not seed o'clock fix. Six o'clock feed.

*The baby cries again.*

BARRY   (*motionless: eyes closed again*) Coming, sweetheart, Daddy coming.

GLENDA   (*beginning to waken, fearfully*) Is it two o'clock? Please God, let it only be two o'clock ... I'll never want for anything again ...

BARRY   You *did* the two o'clock ...

GLENDA   (*almost in tears before she's even opened her eyes*) Did I?

BARRY   At two o'clock.

GLENDA   Make a cup of tea, love.

BARRY   I thought perhaps I might go back to sleep.

GLENDA   I begged you to buy a teasmaid. I begged.

BARRY   (*opening his eyes: lying staring at the ceiling*) What happens is, my brain turns to porridge. Then it starts moving. Very slowly moving porridge.

*The baby's cries become stronger.*

GLENDA  Barry!

*Barry sighs and hoists himself out of bed.*

BARRY  Alright, Piggle-Poggle, Daddy's here.
GLENDA  (*disgusted, exhausted*) Piggle-Poggle . . .
BARRY  Coming, Chumley-Bumley! Little Pipsqueak.
GLENDA  Barry? Who's little Pipsqueak?
BARRY  Glenda, don't start. I'm not awake yet.
GLENDA  I only said who's Pipsqueak?
BARRY  (*irritatedly*) Oh, God, oh, Montreal!
GLENDA  Who's Pipsqueak, Barry?
BARRY  Forget it!
GLENDA  I take it you mean 'Darren'? If you *mean* Darren, why don't you *say* Darren? It's his name.
BARRY  Is it?
GLENDA  I'm not arguing, Barry!
BARRY  You do a damn good impersonation!

*The baby cries.*

GLENDA  Daddy coming, Darren, darling!
BARRY  Coming, Jason!
GLENDA  We're not calling him Jason!
BARRY  We're certainly not calling him bloody Darren!
GLENDA  We are! I've got post-natal depression!

*Her yell is topped by the baby's screams of hunger.*


## 2 Miss Shepherd's kitchen

*Miss Shepherd is in her dressing gown, preparing a mug of tea for herself. She's waiting for the kettle to boil.*

*She's singing sleepily, but very happily to herself. Some quaintly incongruous pop song.*

*She glances at a wall-calendar. Cut to see one date ringed in red. She smiles happily at the date.*


## 3 Stan's bedsitter

*The room is in half-darkness.*

*Stan and his girlfriend, Liz, are lying back to back in bed. They're both lying there wide awake and worried. Both under the impression that the other is asleep.*

110

*After a few moments, Liz begins to pretend to snore. She waits a moment between each snore to see if she's succeeded in waking Stan. He, in turn, listens carefully, wondering if he can use the snoring as an excuse officially to wake up. (Which, of course, is what Liz wants.)*

*After two or three more 'snores' –*

STAN  (*tentatively*) Liz! (*She snores again*) Hey, Liz!

LIZ  (*Stirring and pretending to grunt, sleepily*) I'm asleep.

STAN  You were snoring. You woke me up. I was fast asleep.

LIZ  *I* was. I'll bring you a nice cup of tea in bed.

STAN  *I* should do it, this morning.

LIZ  *Tomorrow* morning. We'll be husband and wife tomorrow morning.

*Which is precisely what – unknown to the other – has been worrying them both sick all night long. A pause while they both lie there, sick with fear.*

STAN  Dead to the world, I was. Then you started this snoring.

LIZ  I must've been in this really deep sleep. You know, really zonked.

STAN  *I* was.

LIZ  And me.

*A pause. They lie there, tired out and worried sick; the butterflies in their stomachs beginning to rouse themselves for an extremely busy day.*

LIZ  (*worriedly*) Happy?

STAN  (*worriedly*) I'll say. You?

LIZ  (*worriedly*) 'Course.

## 4  Miss Shepherd's kitchen

*Miss Shepherd is at the table, finishing her tea and toast, singing through each mouthful. She takes the slice of bread to the door, opens it, and starts throwing breadcrumbs into the garden.*

MISS S  Breakfast, lads! Big day today! Treat yourselves to a worm sandwich.

*She hums happily to herself.*

## 5  Mr Crabtree's living room

*Mr Crabtree, in crumpled pyjamas, and looking as though he's been sleeping in a chair all night (which he has) is tottering across the room from the kitchen, with a teapot in his hand. He opens the living room door and calls upstairs.*

MR C Doctor? Doctor Benson? How much sugar do you take?

DOCTOR *(coming down the stairs)* I'm coming down.

MR C Fair enough. Only I'm just making a brew, with all due respect. I was wondering how much sugar you . . .

*He stands aside as the doctor enters.*

DOCTOR None, thanks, Mr Crabtree. *(He looks at Mr Crabtree soberly, kindly)* I suggest you have a good strong cup. Very sweet.

*Mr Crabtree looks at him – and understands what's happened.*

MR C *(subdued)* Like that, eh?

DOCTOR I'm afraid so.

MR C Yes.

*A quiet pause.*

DOCTOR It was very peaceful.

MR C Doesn't sound like Clara.

*The doctor smiles slightly, in spite of the situation.*

MR C Did she have any last words?

DOCTOR Sorry.

MR C I don't think it *could've* been Clara.

DOCTOR She didn't actually regain consciousness.

MR C No. She wouldn't once she'd set her mind to it.

DOCTOR Sit down and drink your tea, Mr Crabtree. *(They go towards the table)* I'll leave you some sedatives before I go.

*They sit at the table. Mr Cratbtree sits staring into space. The doctor pours out a cup of tea for him.*

MR C *(calmly, quietly)* By hell, eh? No more Clara. I sat in her chair there all night . . . while you were up with her. Pins and needles giving me jip. Daft stuff that goes through your head . . . In the old days if a neighbour gave us a bit of chicken for Christmas dinner she used to make me pull the wishbone with her. And *cheat*. So's she always won. Then she'd say 'Guess what I wished' and I'd say 'What?' And she'd say 'That you'd mind your own business'. *(Pause, sighs)* Gone, but not forgotten . . .

DOCTOR *(smiling, puzzled)* I should hope not . . .

MR C  Eh?

DOCTOR  She's only just this minute gone!

MR C  (*realises what he's said*) Oh, I see. (*Pause*) Mind you, she always said she wouldn't go at *all*. She used to turn to me and say 'I'll never go before you, Walter'. (*Pause*) Well, words to that effect. What she mostly said was 'I'll see you six feet under first, you old bugger!'

*Sighs. Rolls his pyjama leg up and turns to the doctor.*

MR C  Could you cast your eye over my leg while you're here?

## 6  Inside travelling car

*Miss Shepherd is driving along suburban streets in her old, but spotless Morris Minor. The radio is playing pop music. Although very vague about the actual words of the song, Miss Sheperd is singing (almost) in unison with it.*

RADIO DJ  You're listening to the Tony Blackburn show . . .

MISS S  (*equably*) Well, you sock it to me, Anthony . . .

*She resumes singing with the record.*

## 7  Barry's and Glenda's kitchen

*The same pop song is playing on the transistor radio.*

*Glenda is taking washed nappies from the washing-machine and hanging them on a plastic clothes-horse. She's wearing her dressing gown. Barry, fully dressed, is eating his breakfast while reading The Daily Telegraph. They're evidently still annoyed about their 6 a.m. skirmish, and making as much noise as possible from hanging nappies and turning a newspaper's pages. Suddenly:*

GLENDA  Ssshhh!

BARRY  He can't be awake. He's only just gone to sleep.

GLENDA  (*the opportunity she was angling for*) Who has?

BARRY  Here we go!

GLENDA  Darren, you mean?

*Barry sighs, realising what she's on about.*

BARRY  Oh, God, Oh, Montreal . . . (*calmly*) Have you ever seen a man driven mad? They kill. They go straight for the throat and kill. I've seen it on the Labour Relations Committee.

GLENDA  Forty-two days old – and he hasn't got a name!!

BARRY  We're allowed forty-two days! He'll get one today! Lunchtime. I shall go to the Register Office at lunchtime.

GLENDA  And call him what?

BARRY  You *know* what.

*Glenda reaches an agonised compromise.*

GLENDA  Barry. If I drop Darren, will you drop bloody Jason?

BARRY  (*sighing*) And call him what?

GLENDA  Hang on.

*She races into the living room.*

BARRY  (*yelling after her*) Not again! Not that bloody book again! I know them by heart, Glenda! Abe, Abel, Abloyc, Abner, Abraham, Absolom, Adam, Adrian, Alastair, Albany, Albert, Aldous, Alexander, Alfred, Banquo, Barclay, Beavis, Bruno . . .

*The baby starts crying. Barry immediately freezes. Glenda, who's re-entering, also freezes. They both stare towards the garden. The baby goes silent. They both unfreeze. Glenda holds a paperback book of boys' names.*

BARRY  (*loud whisper*) Glenda. Love. There isn't time to go through all that lot again. It's got to be today. By law.

GLENDA  I'll shut my eyes and open it at random.

BARRY  It doesn't work. You've done it every day since you were three minutes pregnant.

GLENDA  The very last time.

BARRY  (*sighing wearily*) It it opens on Kenneth, you knew a Kenneth at Table Tennis Club, and you didn't like him. If it opens on Jeremy, you knew a Jeremy at night school – or in a previous life – and you didn't like him. If it opens on a . . .

*Glenda has meanwhile closed her eyes, opened the book at random, then opened her eyes again.*

BARRY  Well?

GLENDA  (*closing the book*) Forget it.

BARRY  Someone else you don't like?

GLENDA  'Barry'.

BARRY  *My* name's Barry!

*She gives him a fractional, wan smile.*

## 8 An open-air car park

*Miss Shepherd drives her car in and parks. She gets out and calls across to Dan, an elderly attendant, who's about to start washing another car.*

MISS S  Good morning, Dan!

DAN  What's good about it?

MISS S  It's Thursday!

*She locks the car, and walks jauntily towards the gate. Dan has meanwhile been deep in thought – then finally –*

DAN  What's good about Thursdays?

MISS S  Not *all* Thursdays. *This* one.

*She beams at him, happily, and continues on her way through the gate. He watches her go, still puzzled.*

DAN  And what's good about *this* one, then?

MISS S  (*turning and smiling conspiratorially*) Ah!

*She continues on her way. Dan returns to his car-washing preparations.*

DAN  (*to himself*) Fridays are alright. (*Pause*) It's cod and chips, Fridays.

## 9 Stan's bedsitter

*Stan is shaving at the sink. Liz is ironing her two-piece suit. Their nervous nausea is intensifying by the minute. With nothing to talk about except their impending marriage, they're in a gently-manic philosophic mood.*

STAN  Do you know what an apprentice said at work?

LIZ  (*apprehensively*) About getting married?

STAN  No. He's only a kid.

LIZ  (*subsiding again*) Oh.

STAN  He said the Beatles were the best group there's ever been. Bar none.

LIZ  (*not interested*) Oh.

*A pause. Stan continues shaving, Liz continues ironing.*

STAN  So then I said 'What about the Rolling Stones, then?' And he said 'Who?' And I said 'The Rolling Stones'. And he'd never heard of them.

115

LIZ  (*not interested*) Blimey.

STAN  You never think of that, do you? That, you know, youngsters are coming up, like, while you're ... (*pause*) I felt as though I was my dad ...

*A silence. They continue with their preparations.*

LIZ  You never hear much about flying saucers these days.

STAN  (*unsure, puzzled*) The group?

LIZ  *Is* there a group?

STAND  I don't think so ...

LIZ  From outer space. Flying saucers.

STAN  Oh.

LIZ  There used to be a whole *thing* about them a year or two back. In magazines.

STAND  Yes.

*The subject seems exhausted. A new wave of nerves starts to overtake them.*

STAND  You OK?

LIZ  Fine. You?

STAN  Great.

*Pause*

LIZ  Sandra Dalton at work once thought she saw a flying saucer. Mind you, she once thought she saw Jesus. She didn't buy 'Playgirl' for six months after that ... (*Looks at her iron, puzzled. Then notices it's not plugged in*) Typical ...

## 10 Outside the register office

*Miss Shepherd approaches and goes into the building. We stay on the plaque at the door to establish 'Register Office for Births, Marriages and Deaths', and the names and titles of the personnel who work there.*

## 11 Mr Crabtree's living room

*The doctor is seated at the table, writing out a prescription. (Clara's death certificate and medical card are to one side.)*

    *Mr Crabtree enters from upstairs. Now wearing trousers and braces over the top of his pyjamas.*

DOCTOR  All done, Mr Crabtree.

MR C  Nearly. Apart from my shave. I'll have my shave after.

DOCTOR   No ... all *this*. (*Indicates documents*) All done.

MR C   Oh, I see. I like to give the hairs an hour or two's daylight. Then I take 'em by surprise.

DOCTOR   (*showing documents*) Death certificate for your good lady. Prescription for your lumbago. And one for more sedatives if needed.

MR C   Thank you.

DOCTOR   And thank *you* for the tea.

MR C   Thank you.

*The doctor starts gathering his things together to leave.*

MR C   Would you like a piece of chewing gum?

DOCKTOR   No, thanks.

MR C   (*unwrapping a piece of chewing gum for himself*) I gave up smoking. At Clara's behest.

DOCTOR   It'll be quiet without her, I expect ...

MR C   By hell.

DOCTOR   You'll miss her. It's only natural. But in time ...

MR C   They'll all miss her. I shouldn't be surprised if the bingo hall goes into liquidation.

DOCTOR   Enjoyed a game, did she?

MR C   She had a pencil twelve inches long. They gave it her for good attendance. She was a *lady*, was Clara. I mean ... *anyone* can have a vicious nature. It's only human. No one's saying she was perfect. She gave the rent chap a lacerated nostril.

DOCTOR   A what?

MR C   Stuck her bingo pencil up it. He was always a bit off-hand with her after that. *Polite*, but, you know, kept himself to himself more.

*The doctor gets his coat on and makes for the door.*

DOCTOR   Well, you've got yourself to think of now, Mr Crabtree.

MR C   I can but try.

DOCTOR   And you'll take the Death Certificate and her Medical Card to the Register Office, won't you?

MR C   If that's what she wanted.

DOCTOR   (*thrown: puzzled*) Well, I'm not so sure *she* did ...

MR C   I've always done my duty. You can check that in my army records. Under Lancashire Fusiliers.

DOCTOR   (*at the door*) It's ... um ... it's on Gladstone Street. The Register Office.

MR C   I'll be there. I'm that sort of feller. Do anything for anyone.
Distance no object. I'll get a taxi for my leg. She was well
insured.

## 12   Miss Shepherd's office

*Jenny, a young clerical assistant, is at her tiny desk, reading
horoscopes in 'Vogue'.*

   *Miss Shepherd enters ebulliently, still singing to herself – then stops
dead in her tracks.*

   *Her happiness drains instantly away as she stares in horrified
disbelief at her extremely old and rickety desk which stands in the
middle of the room, just as it has for the last two or three decades.*

MISS S   Where is it?

JENNY   (*apprehensive of Miss Shepherd's disappointment*) It hasn't come
yet.

MISS S   They said first thing Thursday morning! Before office hours!

JENNY   It just hasn't come just yet.

MISS S   They *promised*!

JENNY   I'll put the kettle on.

*She gets up to attend to the kettle, milk, etc., which are on a window
ledge.*

MISS S   (*flatly*) Morning, Jenny.

JENNY   Morning, Miss Shepherd.

*Miss Shepherd flops deflated into a straight-backed chair next to
Jenny's desk.*

   *She sits glowering at her own desk.*

MISS S   Well, I'm not sitting behind *that* desk again! Not one more
day. Not another minute. (*sighs*) They promised
faithfully . . .

JENNY   It was the same with my phone extension. Eight months that
took.

MISS S   I've been waiting since the day I came!! Fourteen years!
Look at the damn thing. Mr Talbot, before me, no doubt
waited *fifty* years! God knows who had it before *him*!
Methuselah.

*She suddenly leaps up and grabs the 'phone on her own desk.*

MISS S   (*into 'phone*) Town Clerk, please! (*Pause, then to Jenny*) I was
up at six this morning. I haven't been up at six since I was a

118

kid. The Girl Guides trip to Harrogate. (*Pause*) And *singing*. Songs I didn't even know I knew . . .

JENNY   I *cried* about the 'phone extension. I used to go home and cry . . .

MISS S   (*briskly, into 'phone*) Good morning, is he there, please? (*Pause*) Miss Shepherd, Superintendent of Marriages, Deputy Registrar Births and Deaths. (*Pause*) I see. Well, when he does condescend to waddle into his office – (*Pause*) 'Waddle'. W, A, double D, L, E – could you kindly tell him I rang, and shall continue to ring every hour, on the hour, 'til he goes even *balder*? (*Pause*) Pardon? (*Pause*) Certainly. It's in connection with my non-existent new desk, Stationery Requisition Order Number B534, submitted to you April, 17th, and subsequently ignored 'til I finally threw a tantrum in his office three weeks ago in front of a Norwegian visitor to Britain, and subsequently ignored again it seems.

JENNY   (*whispering*) Tea or coffee?

MISS S   (*into 'phone*) Yes, he did. Verbally, in the presence of my clerical assistant last week. 'Thursday without fail'. It's now Thursday, and he's failed. (*Pause*) Thank you. Please do. (*She replaces the receiver*)

JENNY   Tea or coffee?

MISS S   Yes, please (*preoccupied with thoughts*)

JENNY   Which?

MISS S   Whichever's easier.

JENNY   Makes no difference.

MISS S   (*momentarily irritated*) Either, then, Jenny!

JENNY   Tea, then.

MISS S   Coffee, I think.

JENNY   Coffee.

*Jenny continues preparing the coffee. Miss Shepherd flops down, exhausted, in her own chair at her own desk. She sits looking at the desk. Resentfully.*

MISS S   (*calmly, almost bored, matter-of-fact*) The *other* drawer jammed yesterday. The one with the key already broken in the lock. With a Granny Smith and a banana inside. They'll go rancid. One day this desk'll get up and stagger out into the sunset on its own. Keep your fingers crossed.

JENNY   (*profoundly, wisely*) The worst thing about being disappointed is if you've been looking forward to something . . .

119

MISS S  (*puzzled*) What?

JENNY  (*unsure herself of what she's talking about*) Anyway, it's heartbreaking.

MISS S  (*subdued*) It's probably the very least heartbreaking thing in the world. The least important. The least anything. (*Pause*) And it's all I think about.


### 13  A post-natal clinic

*Four or five prams (uninhabited) are parked outside the entrance. Glenda approaches wheeling her pram. She stands, rocking the pram, ostensibly to rock her baby to sleep, but actually as an excuse to lie in wait for other mothers and their babies to appear.*

*First mother emerges from the clinic. Carrying her baby. She starts putting the baby into its pram. Glenda nonchalantly sidles up, wheeling her pram. She peers at first mother's baby.*

GLENDA  Aaah! Isn't she beautiful!

FIRST M  *He.*

GLENDA  Oh. Sorry. Of course. (*To baby*) Hello, little man! And what's *your* name, then?

FIRST M  Jason.

GLENDA  (*face falling*) Oh. Nice.

FIRST M  (*proudly*) Well, he looks a Jason, really, doesn't he?

GLENDA  Yes. He does a bit.

FIRST M  And he's put on seven ounces, haven't you, darling? There are two other Jasons in there – and they've only put on six and three quarters.

GLENDA  Oh. Lovely.

*First mother continues organising the baby in its pram. Second mother approaches, wheeling her pram down the street towards the clinic. Glenda again nonchalantly lies in wait for her, then peers into the pram.*

GLENDA  Aaahh! Isn't he gorgeous!

SECOND M  (*proudly*) Thank you. He's on solids.

GLENDA  Aaahhh . . .

SECOND M  He's ever so bright. He knows just what you mean if you say 'Naughty. Mustn't touch. Mummy thump!'

GLENDA  (*smile freezing*) Sweet. The little love. And what's his little name?

SECOND M  Christopher Bartholomew.

120

GLENDA   (*dubiously*) Nice. I used to know a Christopher at the Rugby Club dances, but he wasn't a *bit* . . .

SECOND M   My husband only wanted to call the poor thing 'Darren', didn't he?

GLENDA   (*brightening*) Really?

SECOND M   'Darren', I ask you! Still. What do fathers know? They only get the pleasure.

GLENDA   (*face falling*) Yes.

SECOND M   What's yours called?

GLENDA   Um . . . we haven't given it much thought, actually . . .

SECOND M   Some don't. 'Bye then.

GLENDA   'Bye.

*Second mother wheels her pram away.*

    *Glenda stands for a moment, then wheels her pram away in the opposite direction . . . more worried than ever.*


## 14  Stan's bedsitter

*It's now Stan's turn to do his ironing. He's standing at the ironing board, pressing the trousers of his best suit.*

    *He's wearing the jacket (with a carnation in the buttonhole) over his shirt. Bare legs revealed beneath.*

    *Liz has her hairpiece (which is in curlers) mounted on a wig block. She's drying the curls with a hand hair-dryer.*

    *Both of them are in the same state of nervous nausea as before.*

STAN   The thing is most people have this thing . . . like they have to get married to sort of progress in their relationship . . . I mean . . .

LIZ   What?

STAN   What?

LIZ   I can't hear you. (*She switches off her hair-dryer*)

STAN   No, I'm just saying . . .

LIZ   What?

STAN   Most people think they must get married to sort of cement their relationship . . . whereas *us* for example . . .

LIZ   *What* their relationship?

STAN   Cement.

LIZ   Oh. Yes.

*She switches the dryer back on and continues drying her hairpiece.*

STAN   Whereas we've no need to.

*Liz switches off her dryer.*

LIZ No need to what?
STAN Get married. I mean – we *want* to.
LIZ Yes.

*She switches the hair-dryer on again and continues with her hairpiece.*

STAN It's our *choice*.

*Liz switches off the hair-dryer.*

LIZ Sorry?
STAN I'm just saying – it's our choice.
LIZ We don't have to if we don't want to.
STAN Not at all.

*A pause. Both feeling sick.*

LIZ The stem of your carnation should be on the *outside*.
STAN (*looks at his carnation*) Oh. Right.

*He starts fixing it as it should be. Liz returns to hairdrying.*

## 15 A small sub-post office

*It's pension day. A queue of old-age pensioners are waiting patiently and resignedly to be paid, pension books in hand.*

*At the end of the queue is Mr Crabtree standing next to another old man.*

MR C (*referring to the cashier*) Anyone'd think it was her money, speed she goes at . . .
OLD MAN Typical.
MR C By the time you get out again, prices have gone up another 2p. I blame inflation.

*A pause. They stand there.*

MR C I'm just *single* pension now.
OLD MAN (*not interested*) Oh, yes?
MR C (*self-important nonchalance*) My missus passed away this morning.
OLD MAN Mine's in Doncaster. She goes every two or three . . .
MR C I did all I could. No good just thinking of yourself, is it?
OLD MAN She goes every two or three months. Sees the grandchildren. The eldest is . . .

MR C   Wasn't easy, mind you. She was a bad patient. Bit of a bad bugger all round at times, no disrespect. (*Pause*) I've got the telly and my bowling.

OLD MAN   Yes.

MR C   (*taps his breast pocket*) Death certificate. The doctor's put me in charge of it. Got to take it to town and everything. I shall do my best. That's life, really, isn't it?

OLD MAN   My missus likes going to Doncaster whenever . . .

MR C   Mine passed away this morning.

OLD MAN   Aye.

MR C   You have to try and forget.

## 16  Miss Shepherd's office

*Miss Shepherd is behind her desk, seated. Seated facing her across the desk is Mr Patel, a Pakistani.*

*Jenny is at her desk, sorting out correspondence.*

MISS S   (*very patiently*) Mr Patel, we're not the Inland Revenue, we're the Register Office . . .

MR PATEL   (*quietly seething*) Yes. Old, old story. That isn't what you say when you ask everyone vote for you!

MISS S   Pardon?

MR PATEL   Little papers through the door saying vote, vote, vote, let's make Britain great again!

MISS S   No, you see, all matters of taxation are . . .

MR PATEL   All I'm asking is civil question . . . do I get rebate for my wife?

*Miss Shepherd looks at him, beginning to remember.*

MISS S   Did I superintend the marriage of you and Mrs Patel?

MR PATEL   January 15. Eleven o'clock a.m.

MISS S   Well, of *course* you can claim a tax rebate. You should've claimed it in . . .

MR PATEL   Not for *that* wife.

MISS S   (*puzzled*) Sorry?

MR PATEL   (*amazed she doesn't understand*) For my other wife.

*Jenny and Miss Shepherd exchange an expressionless glance. Miss Shepherd returns attention to Mr Patel.*

MISS S   (*calmly*) *Which* other wife?

*Her hand creeps towards the 'phone.*

MR PATEL  In Karachi.

MISS S  You have *two* wives?

MR PATEL  I'm *allowed* two wives, I'm a Moslem. What I want is two tax rebates.

*Miss Shepherd relaxes, and begins to withdraw her hand from the 'phone.*

MISS S  But the Karachi one isn't subject to British law, she ... (*She checks herself*) Hang on – I'll tell you the best thing ...

*She writes a 'phone number on a piece of paper.*

MISS S  Anything to do with income tax, religion or library books ring that number.

*Jenny stares at her, blankly. Miss Shepherd hands the paper to Mr Patel.*

MR PATEL  Thank you.

MISS S  That's his job.

MR PATEL  (*rising*) Thank you very much, indeed. Good day. (*To Jenny*) Good day, Miss.

MISS S  'Bye, 'bye.

JENNY  'Bye, 'bye.

*He exits.*
*Jenny swivels round to Miss Shepherd.*

JENNY  (*incredulously*) Income tax, religion and library books??? *Whose* job??

MISS S  Town Clerk.

JENNY  He doesn't deal with *any* of them!

MISS S  He doesn't deal with anything! (*She grabs up the 'phone*) (*Into 'phone*) Town Clerk, please. (*Pause*) Thank you. May I speak to him, please? (*Pause*) His wife. (*Pause*) Oh.

*She puts the receiver back into its cradle hastily.*

JENNY  What happened?

MISS S  He's already on the telephone speaking to his wife. (*Sighs*) Bad as Mr Patel ...

*Jenny gets on with her work. Miss Shepherd sits soberly thinking.*

MISS S  Jenny? Do you laugh at me behind my back?

*Jenny stares at her.*

JENNY   What?

MISS S   Don't answer, it was a rhetorical question. (*Pause*) I just wonder if I've gone a bit eccentric without me noticing it. A bit potty. Like Mr Quigley in the Borough Treasurer's Office, lifting off his ginger wig that doesn't fit whenever he says good morning. And Mrs Trent. With her Billy the Bucket and Mary the Mop, saying 'I'm just going to scrub Freddie the Floor'. I just wondered if I'd joined the Happy Band. Do I do other strange things apart from witter on about my desk?

JENNY   Oh, you are daft!

MISS S   (*apprehensively*) Am I?

JENNY   Not daft. *Daft*. It was only that you got over-excited, thinking today's the day. It's nice working for you – it gives me an interest.

MISS S   I sometimes talk to myself. But I know I'm doing it. I thought that made it alright ...

JENNY   *I* talk to myself. I say 'Bear up, Jenny, soon be lunchtime'. Stuff like that.

MISS S   (*worriedly*) I've actually been counting the *days*, though! Ticking them off! If I'm watching a play or something on the telly ... say about police stations or somewhere ... I look at the *desks*! Last Saturday afternoon, I was out shopping and it started pouring down. I was like a drowned rat. And I thought 'Who cares? My new desk comes on Thursday!' And on I squelched. It was like what'sisname in 'Singing in the Rain' ... only he was in *love*, for God's sake ...

JENNY   I remember my Mam wanting a clock with a crinoline lady sat on it for the living room. She was in a dream world for two months while it was on order. She kept burning my Dad's tea – and she didn't even know she'd put it in the oven. The day she got it, she was trembling. She nearly got shingles, my Mam.

*A long pause.*

MISS S   I'll bet your *dad* thought she'd gone potty.

JENNY   He's room to talk. He always carries a raw potato in his jacket for fear.

MISS S   Fear of what?

JENNY   Anything. Phlegm. Me marrying someone with long hair. Him not winning the pools. Everything.

*A long pause.*

*During it, Jenny returns to her work, singing contentedly to herself. Miss Shepherd sits. Quiet. Reflective.*

JENNY (*blithely*) Anyway, it's silly, really, isn't it?

MISS S Mmm?

JENNY Upsetting yourself. I mean, it's only a *desk*, isn't it? You'd only see it at work. A desk's only nine to five. It's not real life. (*Laughs*) Hell's bells! If that's all there was to look forward to in the world! Well, hell's bells!

*She laughs happily. Close on Miss Shepherd. Trying to smile, trying to share the joke.*


## 17 Barry's and Glenda's kitchen

GLENDA (*speaking on the 'phone*) Hello, mother. Glenda. (*Pause*) Just to say hello. (*Pause*) Oh, I'm fine. (*Pause, then tenderly*) Oh, he's fine. (*Pause, then frostily*) And *him*. (*Pause*) Mother, you remember you said you met Mrs Chancey at the Weightwatchers and how her bottom's dropped off and she looks like a pickled herring? Well, you remember you said she said her two grandsons have got lovely names? Well, what were they? (*Pause*) No reason. (*Pause*) Mother, I'm *not* worried about names! (*Pause*) I'm not! (*Pause*) No, Mother, mothers do *not* know everything! I ought to know, *I'm* one. What were they? (*Pause: her face falls*) Kojak and Columbo. (*Pause*) Mmm. Lovely. (*Pause*) What, *ours*? Oh, 'Darren'. Well, probably 'Darren'. (*Pause*) You hate it, don't you? (*Pause*) Don't you? (*Pause*) Mother, you're doing one of your meaningful silences again. (*Pause*) 'How can I tell??' Easy, you're not *saying* anything! (*Pause*) Better go, I'm defrosting the fridge. I only rang to say hello. 'Bye.

*She hangs up, and sits for a moment, worriedly, frustratedly. She picks up the 'phone again and dials.*

GLENDA (*Into 'phone*) May I speak to Mr Edgeley, please, Personnel? (*Pause*) *Mrs* Edgeley. (*Pause*) Barry? (*Pause*) Me. Just saying hello ... Um, incidentally, *what* time are you going to the Register Office? (*Pause*) No reason. (*Pause*) I hope your secretary can't hear that language. Her father *is* a Freemason. (*Pause*) Three o'clock! I thought you said lunchtime? (*Pause*) It wasn't supposed to mean *anything*. 'Bye.

*She hangs up, and immediately dials again.*

GLENDA (*into 'phone*) Hello, mother. Me again. (*Pause*) Can you pop over and look after little Darren, or whoever he is, after I've given him his two o'clock feed? (*Pause*) Just to change him and sing him to sleep? (*Pause*) *Anything* ... 'Land of Hope and Glory' – whatever comes to mind! (*Pause*) Thanks, I'll only be out an hour or so. (*Pause*) Nowhere special.

### 18 Stan's bedsitter

*Stan and Liz are now dressed for their wedding: Stan in pressed suit and correctly pinned carnation, Liz in her two-piece and her hairpiece and a small bouquet. They're both ready to go. The butterflies are doing their worst.*

STAN OK, then?

LIZ Mmm? What? Fine. Yes.

STAN Ready as we'll ever be, eh?

*He laughs nervously. She laughs nervously in reply.*

STAN (*glances at his watch*) Better be off, then, what with the traffic ... (*Looks at his watch again, panicking*) Has it stopped? (*Listens to it*) No. (*To Liz*) I thought perhaps it'd stopped.

LIZ Are they meeting us there?

STAN Traffic may be bad, you never know.

LIZ Are Mick and Mary meeting us there?

STAN Yes. I just said yes.

LIZ You didn't. You said the traffic might be bad.

STAN I never mentioned the traffic, love.

*Liz glances round the room.*

LIZ Now. Have I got everything? Handbag? Yep.

STAN (*patting his pockets*) Wallet, money, confetti in case Mary forgets ... (*looks at his watch again*) If the traffic *isn't* bad, we'll be *early* ...

LIZ Better early than never.

STAN What?

LIZ Right, then.

*They still stand there.*

STAN   Right.

*He crosses the room and picks up two crash helmets (which we see for the first time).*
*He puts his on, and hands the second to Liz.*

LIZ   I'll wash up when we get back.

*They exit.*

### 19  Exterior, main street (daytime)

*Mr Crabtree makes his way busily along the street.*
*A woman shopper is hurriedly rushing down the street with her shopping bag, towards him. He stops her.*

MR C   I'm alright for Gladstone Street, am I? Registry Office?
SHOPPER   (*not interested: intent on getting past him*) I don't know. Sorry.
MR C   Oh, yes, I *am*. It's first left then left again.
SHOPPER   Do you mind! I've my shopping to do?

*She manages to get past him.*

MR C   It's my wife, you see. Passed away this morning. Official. Merciful release, really.
SHOPPER   (*not even looking back at him*) Only the shops close in ten minutes!

*She hurries off on her way.*
*Mr Crabtree walks on, importantly, in the opposite direction towards Gladstone Street.*

### 20  Miss Shepherd's office

*Jenny is at her desk, writing addresses on envelopes. Miss Shepherd sits at her desk, mechanically toying with papers ... her mind sadly on her disappointment. There is a knock at the door. They both react with sudden excitement.*

MISS S   Come in.
JENNY   Come in!

*A window cleaner in overalls pops his head in.*

WINDOW C   Is this the right office!
MISS S   Are you collecting a desk?
WINDOW C   Eh?

MISS S    Sorry?

WINDOW C    Do you do babies in here?

*Miss Shepherd's and Jenny's excitement fades.*

JENNY    The registrar's office. Next door.

MISS S    I'm his deputy. Can I . . .?

WINDOW C    Oh, not *now*. I'm cleaning the windows now. The wife'll come when she's out of hospital. Eight pound 3 ounces, 4 o'clock this morning, both doing well. No, I just wanted to enquire as to if there's a limit.

MISS S    (*blanky*) If there's a limit . . .

WINDOW C    As to how many.

MISS S    Babies?

WINDOW C    Names. We want to call him Boulton, Thomas, Todd, Daniel, McFarland, Nish . . .

MISS S    Rioch, Gemill, Newton, Davies, Hector and Lee.

WINDOW C    (*flabbergasted*) Bloody hell . . .

MISS S    Derby Football Club.

WINDOW C    Are you a supporter?

MISS S    You're not the first. It happens every season. It's usually the Liverpool team even when they *don't* win the Championship. It used to be Manchester United once upon a time. Not now though. Don't know why . . .

*The 'phone rings abruptly.*

MISS S    (*barely suppressed excitement*) Excuse me.

*She grasps her 'phone quickly, before Jenny can pick up hers.*

MISS C    (*into 'phone, excitedly*) Miss Shepherd speaking, yes?? (*Pause, then disappointed*) Oh, right. (*To Jenny*) It's for you.

*She replaces the 'phone as Jenny picks up hers. And sighs.*

MISS S    (*to window cleaner*) Actually. I'm a Sheffield Wednesday supporter.

WINDOW C    They were relegated.

MISS S    Yes.

### 21   The corridor adjacent to Miss Shepherd's office

*Along much of the length of the corridor is a long bench. Seated on it are Barry, Stan and Liz, and Mr Crabtree. Barry is reading a newspaper. He seems calm, confident, a man whose mind is made up.*

*Stan and Liz sit frozen in fear, staring ahead. Mr Crabtree checks the documents in his pension book, then replaces them in his pocket. He takes a piece of chewing gum from his mouth and sticks it under the bench. No one notices. He puts a new piece in his mouth.*

*Jenny pops her head out of Miss Shepherd's office.*

JENNY   Anyone here for the registrar?

BARRY   Here.

STAN   Marriage. (*The word comes out as hardly more than a squeak. He says it again*) Marriage.

JENNY   (*to Barry, indicating the next door*) Have you tried his office?

BARRY   People in.

JENNY   This way then, please.

*Barry gets up and starts towards the door of Miss Shepherd's office. Glenda enters from the street. Barry sees her. His face falls.*

BARRY   Oh, God, Oh, Montreal . . .!

GLENDA   You can say that again.

*She joins him to go into the office.*

## 22  Miss Shepherd's office

*Miss Shepherd is at her desk. Jenny ushers in Glenda and Barry.*

JENNY   Miss Shepherd, deputy registrar.

BARRY/
GLENDA   Good afternoon. Mr and Mrs Edgeley.

MISS S   Good afternoon. Do sit down.

BARRY/
GLENDA   Thank you.

*They sit.*

MISS S   Now what can I . . .?

BARRY   We'd like to . . . (*brief, bitter glance at Glenda*) . . . um, well, register a birth, really.

MISS S   Fine. (*She takes her ledger of births*) You are the parents?

GLENDA   We are.

MISS S   Now, where was the baby born, please?

BARRY   St Theresa's Clinic.

GLENDA   Maternity ward.

MISS S   Er . . . yes. And on what date?

BARRY   29.6.75

MISS S   Thank you. (*To Jenny*) Hospital notification, dear, please. St Theresa's 29th June.

*Jenny starts to get the notification from a file. Barry and Glenda sit staring ahead, po-faced. Jenny gives Miss Shepherd the document. Miss Shepherd prepares to fill in the forms.*

MISS S   And . . . (*Barry and Glenda tense themselves*) . . . what are you calling the baby?

*A tiny pause. Glenda and Barry glance quickly at each other, then away again.*

GLENDA   (*her firm resolve suddenly faltering*) Well, we thought Darren, actually.

BARRY   (*confidence suddenly ebbing*) Or Jason.

MISS S   (*beginning to write*) Darren, Jason . . .

BARRY   (*uncomfortably*) No, no! . . . Um . . . Just Jason.

MISS S   (*to Glenda, puzzled*) I thought *you* said . . .?

GLENDA   (*uncomfortably*) I did. (*Pause*) That is . . . yes, I did.

*A pause. Miss Shepherd puts down her pen and sits back.*

MISS S   Well now. Problem.

*Glenda and Barry look as though they'd like to die.*

GLENDA   Sort of. Yes.

BARRY   In a sense. (*To Glenda*) Perhaps we should've discussed this a little at home . . .

GLENDA   (*almost ready to cry*) We've discussed nothing *else* . . .

BARRY   No. True.

GLENDA   The . . . um . . . the thing is, Miss Shepherd . . . well, it's the child that matters, it's *his* . . . look, I'm very sorry about all this, it's hardly *your* . . . but, well, it's *his life*, isn't it?

BARRY   In a sense.

GLENDA   (*bitterly, to Barry*) Every little boy in England's called Jason!!

BARRY   (*Trying to appear reasonable in the midst of his embarrassment*) Not entirely *every* boy, Glenda. I think you'll find just over fifty per cent are called Darren. (*To Miss Shepherd*) I do apologise . . . We . . . God, it's embarrassing . . . Personally, I'm embarrassed, I am. I'm embarrassed. I find it embarrassing.

*Miss Shepherd, long-experienced, knows he's the one who'll weaken. She starts her long-practised con-trick.*

131

MISS S  May I make a suggestion, Mrs Edgeley?

GLENDA  We've been through every name you can possibly . . .

MISS S  Give way.

*Glenda stares at her.*

GLENDA  Pardon?

*Suddenly, loudly, we hear the strains of a mouth organ playing 'Get me to the Church on time' – badly.*
*Miss Shepherd and Jenny look at each other, wearily.*

MISS S  Go on, Jen. Whoever it is, threaten him with bye-law 17, sub-section 12.

JENNY  What's that?

MISS S  I've no idea. It works though.

*Jenny gets up to exit. Miss Shepherd turns back to Barry and Glenda and smiles.*

MISS S  We always get one. Some hooligan with a carnation in his buttonhole. Some little Jason or Darren twenty years on . . .

## 23 The corridor

*Stan and Liz are sitting there . . . their nervous agony now compounded by their mouth-organ-playing witness, Mick. With them is their second witness, Mick's girlfriend, Mary. Stan and Liz are trying to make Mick stop playing. Mary's enjoying the tune.*
*Still in his place, in his own little world, paying them no attention at all, is Mr Crabtree.*

STAN  Shush, Mick! Quit it! You'll get us turfed out!

LIZ  Mary! Tell him!

*Mick dodges them and continues playing. Jenny approaches from Miss Shepherd's office.*

JENNY  Excuse me, please. We haven't a music licence for this corridor. Music isn't allowed.

MICK  Come off it, sweetheart! It's a big day!

JENNY  Not everywhere.

MICK  They're getting married!

JENNY  Yes, well, *we've important* things to do. Sorry – bye-law 17, sub-section 12.

132

MICK  And what's that say?

JENNY  It just *does*, that's all. So cool it.

*She returns to Miss Shepherd's office. Mick pockets his mouth-organ.*

## 24  Miss Shepherd's office

*Miss Shepherd, Barry and Glenda as before.*
*Jenny re-enters and sits down. Glenda, crushed, is staring at Miss Shepherd.*

GLENDA  Don't you like Darren?

MISS S  I think Darren's fine. *And* Jason. But, for the sake of the baby, I suggest ...

GLENDA  (*wildly*) It's me that *had* the baby! I *grew* him! I had the backache and the wobbly legs and the ... (*petering out*) ... well, *ladies'* things ...

*A short, embarrassed moment. Barry swallows.*

BARRY  (*to Miss Shepherd, quietly, agonised*) Darren. We'll call him Darren, please. Darren Edgeley. And we're sorry to have troubled you.

*Glenda looks at him, deeply moved.*

GLENDA  Barry ...

BARRY  (*to Miss Shepherd*) And then we'll go.

GLENDA  Barry, that's fantastic ...

BARRY  It's right, that's all. It's the right thing to do.

*Glenda looks at Miss Shepherd to share her emotion.*
*Miss Shepherd winks at her, instead. Glenda looks back at Barry.*

GLENDA  It isn't at all. It was emotional blackmail. I ought to know. I do it all the time. I could take exams in it.

*Miss Shepherd sighs: her trick's rebounded.*

BARRY  You're his mother.

GLENDA  A boy's father's *special*. A boy's father's the one that ... well, he's ...

*A pause. Miss Shepherd looks from one to the other, patiently.*

BARRY  I'd get used to Darren in time.

GLENDA  People can get used to *anything*! I'd even get used to Jason.

BARRY   Glenda, we've to decide *now*! The 42 days are up today! Heads might roll at Somerset House! . . .

MISS S   Actually, between you and me, you've got up to a year. And it isn't Somerset House any more. It's St Catherine's House, Kingsway. There's very little that's sacred.

GLENDA   A year??

MISS S   We can register him without a name. Then sometime within the year we add the name by baptism or certificate of naming.

*Glenda and Barry look at each other, washed in relief.*

GLENDA   We've got a year . . .!

BARRY   We'll come up with something. We'll discuss it. Go into it fully.

GLENDA   We'll find a nice one.

BARRY   A nice name.

GLENDA   Yes.

BARRY   No need to rush it.

GLENDA   None at all

BARRY   Thank you, Miss Shepherd.

MISS S   That's what I'm here for. (*Thinks*) No, I'm not. Anyway, don't mention it. Now . . . (*she returns to the form which still has to be filled in*) . . . the *easy* bit. May I have *your* full name, please, Mr Edgeley?

### 25   The corridor

*Stan and Liz sitting there . . . numb. Mick and Mary sitting beside them . . . bored.*

*Mr Crabtree, sitting, head slumped on chest, having a snooze.*

*Barry and Glenda emerge from Miss Shepherd's office, saying their goodbyes. Barry holds the birth certificate in his hand. They make towards the street exit.*

BARRY   (*glancing at the certificate*) Looks funny without a name . . .

GLENDA   'Adam's' quite nice, actually, isn't it? As a name.

BARRY   Or Damion, possibly.

GLENDA   (*extremely unsure*) Damion?

BARRY   As a possibility.

GLENDA   I used to know a Damion at the hairdresser's. His eyes were terribly close together . . .

*They exit into street.*

## 26  Miss Shepherd's office

MISS S  What's next? Selections from Gilbert and Sullivan?

JENNY  Solemnisation of marriage, should be. Turnbull and Latham.

MISS S  Good. (*She gets to her feet, slowly. Wearily.*) I know every grain of wood in this desk. Like every line in my own face. Maybe that's what's wrong. Like seeing your whole life in a mirror ... (*Lightly*) must be a moral there somewhere ... (*She starts for the door, with ledgers*)
Anyway, see you both soon. (*She exits*)

## 27  The corridor

*Stan, Liz, Mick, Mary and Mr Crabtree, as they appear in scene 25. Miss Shepherd emerges from her office.*

MISS S  (*to Stan and Liz, Mick and Mary*) Um ... Mr Turnbull and Miss Latham?

STAN  (*rising like a bullet in a state of shock*) Yes, thank you!

LIZ  (*also jumping*) Present.

MISS S  (*amiably*) Yes, I remember. Would you come this way, please? (*Mick and Mary also get to their feet*) Um ...just the happy couple for the moment, please.

STAN  (*worriedly*) He didn't know it wasn't allowed. He won't play it again.

MISS S  It's not that. We've the sordid details for a minute or two first ... Paying for your licence and so on ...

STAN  Oh. Right.

*Miss Shepherd knocks on the registrar's door and opens it.*

MISS S  Can I borrow you for a marriage, please Mr Matthews?

LIZ  (*to Stan*) You brought your wallet, did you?

STAN  (*tapping his breast pocket*) Yeah.

MISS S  This way, please.

*She exits into the 'marriage room'. Stan and Liz start to follow her.*

STAN  (*to Liz*) I told you before we left the flat I'd brought it!

LIZ  No, well, I've some money if you didn't.

STAN  I did! I did! (*To Mick and Mary*) See you in a sec.

MARY  Yeah! Don't do anything we wouldn't!

*Mick and Mary hugely enjoy the wittiness of Mary's remark.*

*Stan and Liz follow Miss Shepherd into the marriage room like zombies. Mr Matthews, the registrar, emerges from his office, carrying ledgers and goes through into the marriage room, and closes the door behind him. A pause.*

MARY Bit quiet, weren't they?

MICK Do you know what *I* think it is?

MARY What?

MICK Nerves.

MARY (*giving the thought consideration*) It's a point of view. Could be.

*Mick turns to Mr Crabtree, who's now awake again, clicking his dry tongue round his mouth a little.*

MICK Left you in the lurch, has she?

MR C Eh?

MICK Your blushing bride? Done a bunk, has she?

MR C (*no idea what Mick's talking about*) Aye.

*Mick nods in amused agreement.*
*A pause.*
*Mr Crabtree ponders on Mick's question and turns back to him.*

MR C I'm not here to get married.

MICK No?

MR C I'm here on other business

MICK Very good.

MR I made a special journey.

*Stan pops his head round the marriage room door.*

STAN (*stage whisper to Mick*) We're kicking off.

MICK You little devil.

*Stan disappears inside again. Mick and Mary exit into the marriage room.*

## 28 The 'marriage room'

*Miss Shepherd stands behind a desk on which there is a vase of fresh flowers and a cushion.*
*Facing the desk are two or three rows of straightbacked chairs. Liz is seated on a chair in the front row.*
*Mr Matthews, the registrar, sits at a smaller desk to one side. During the ceremony, he'll be making occasional entries in his register.*

*Stan enters, followed by Mick and Mary. Stan sits next to Liz, while Mick and Mary noisily find seats on the row behind them. When they're settled, Miss Shepherd begins.*

MISS S First of all, may I welcome you to this office, which has been duly sanctioned, according to law, for the celebration of marriage. (*To Stan and Liz*) Will you both stand up, please?

*They do so, albeit not too steadily.*

MISS S Who has the ring, please?
STAN Him.
MICK Me.
MISS S Will you pop it on the cushion, please? (*Mick does so*) Lovely. Now. Stanley and Elizabeth, before joining you in matrimony, it's my duty to remind you both of the solemn and binding character of the vows you are about to make.

*Which is all they need: however frozen their expression – or even smile – they look as though they're about to throw up any second now.*

MISS S Marriage, according to the law of this country, is the union of one man with one woman, voluntarily entered into for life to the exclusion of all others. You understand?

*They nod, woodenly.*

MISS S Now, Stanley, repeat this declaration after me. (*She reads from a small card*) 'I do solemnly declare . . .'

*Stan opens his mouth to speak: nothing comes out.*

LIZ (*loud whisper: prompting him*) I do solemnly declare . . .
MISS S Stanley, first.
LIZ I was helping him.
MISS S Ah.
STAN I do solemnly declare . . .
MISS S That I know not of any lawful impediment . . .
STAN That I know not of any unlawful impedient . . .
MISS S *Lawful* impediment.
STAN Unlawful impediment . . .
MISS S No, Stanley. Of any *lawful*, not *unlawful*.
STAN Lawful impediment.
MISS S That's right.
LIZ (*encouragingly*) Very good, love.
MISS S Why, I, Stanley Turnbull . . .

LIZ (*prompting him*) Stanley Turnbull . . .

STAN Why, I, Stanley Turnbull . . .

### 29 The corridor

*Mr Crabtree as before. He takes the documents from his pocket, satisfies himself they're there and puts them back in his pocket.*
*The window cleaner passes, with his bucket.*

MR C I *was* married, mind you.

WINDOW C You what?

MR C Chapel wedding. Can't remember much about it now. Bar my earhole was itchy all through the service and I couldn't scratch. I remember *that*.

WINDOW C (*moving on*) That's the idea . . .

MR C We had a photo. Hand-painted. God knows where it is now.

### 30 The 'marriage room'

*Miss Shepherd, registrar, Liz, Stan, Mick and Mary, as before.*

LIZ Why, I, Elizabeth Latham . . .

MISS S May not be joined in matrimony . . .

LIZ May not be joined in matrimony . . .

MISS S To Stanley Turnbull.

LIZ To Stanley Turnbull.

MISS S Now take the ring, Stanley, and . . .

LIZ (*a little squeak*) Oh! (*They all look at her*) I think I feel a bit . . . I must have eaten something . . . or something. My stomach feels a bit . . .

STAN (*almost in relief*) Do you want to go to the Ladies? (*To Miss Shepherd*) Actually, I wouldn't mind just visiting the Gents . . . On a temporary basis . . .

MISS S (*amused, sympathetic*) Look, we're very nearly at the end. Any second now, you can go and spend your entire honeymoon in there . . . (*They calm themselves a little*) Don't worry. It's the same for everybody. Everything is. Put the ring on Liz's left hand, third finger.

### 31 The corridor

*Mr Crabtree takes a piece of chewing gum from his mouth, sticks it under the bench, and pops another piece in his mouth.*

## 32  The 'marriage room'

*The ring is now on Liz's finger, Liz and Stan have joined their right hands.*

STAN  Do take thee, Elizabeth Latham . . .

MISS S  To be my *lawful* wedded wife.

STAN  To by my . . . *(an intense effort to get it right)* . . . *lawful* wedded wife.

MISS S  Good. Now, you, Liz. 'I call upon these persons here present . . .'

LIZ  I call upon these persons here present to witness that I, Elizabeth Latham, do take thee, Stanley Turnbull, to be my lawful wedded husband.

MISS S  Great. Now . . .

*Mick immediately launches into Mendelssohn's Wedding March on his mouth organ (raucously and badly).*

MISS S  Please!! It isn't over yet!!!


## 33  The corridor

*In time to the strains of Mendelssohn's Wedding March on Mick's mouth-organ two men in brown overalls are carrying a large, new, modern desk down the corridor.*
*They stop at Miss Shepherd's office door, give a polite kick, and go in with the desk.*


## 34  Miss Shepherd's office

*Jenny sits staring in delight as the men lug the desk in.*
*The Wedding March on Mick's mouth-organ is still audible.*

FIRST MAN  Miss Shepherd's office?

JENNY  Yes! Yes!

FIRST MAN  Mazeltoff.

*They plonk the desk down . . . at the precise moment that the music suddenly stops.*


## 35  The 'marriage room'

*Everyone, except Mary, is looking accusingly at Mick. Abashed, Mick is knocking the spit out of his mouth-organ.*

MISS S *(really annoyed)* Thank you, sir! We do *try* here to give a rather dignified, rather solemn . . .

*Jenny bursts in at the door.*

JENNY *(ecstatic)* Miss Shepherd!

MISS S Jenny!! Do you mind!! Please, this minute, get out of the –

JENNY It's come! The desk! It's come!

> *Miss Shepherd's big, big moment of fulfilment.*
> *A long, wonderful, satisfying pause. She softens.*

MISS S Thank you, Jenny. *(She turns to the others and smiles)* Sorry about that. Now, shall we get you two married off and living happily ever after? 'These declarations, made in the presence of your witnesses, are the ones required by law . . . and henceforth you are man and wife.' *(She grins)* Well done. Congratulations. You may kiss your bride. *(Stan gives Liz a brief peck on the cheek. Miss Shepherd turns to Mick)* And you can murder God Save the Queen all the way to Yates's Wine Lodge.

## 36 The corridor

*Mr Crabtree, now alone on the bench, sits watching the two men in overalls carrying Miss Shepherd's old desk out of her office.*

*Miss Shepherd enters from the marriage room, gives her old desk a passing glance and continues towards her office, slowly and at peace.*

## 37 Miss Shepherd's office

*The new desk stands in position, in all its glory.*

*Jenny sits at her own desk, looking at it, admiringly.*

*Miss Shepherd enters, closes the door behind her, and gazes softly at her desk.*

JENNY *(excitedly)* Well? Gorgeous?

MISS S *(simply, quietly, content)* It's very, very, very, very nice.

*A slight pause . . . then a knock at the door.*

JENNY Come in.

*Mr Crabtree opens the door and pops his head round.*

MR C *(taking documents from his pension book)* Excuse me, only there's only me left. Dr Benson put me in charge of these, with regard to Mrs Clara Crabtree, whom hath passed away this morning.

JENNY  Are you registering a death?

MR C  I've been entrusted with it.

JENNY  You want Mr Matthews, next door. The Registrar.

MISS S  It's alright, Jenny. (*To Mr Crabtree*) Do sit down.

MR C  Thank you.

*He sits. Miss Shepherd and Jenny put small items of desk furniture, ledgers, leaflets, etc., onto her new desk, from wherever they'd been stacked during the changeover.*

MISS S  (*during the above*) Shan't keep you a sec. New desk. Just organising myself.

MR C  That'll be it.

*Miss Shepherd sits and takes her pen and relevant ledger.*

MISS S  Now, do you have the death certificate and medical card?

MR C  Yes, Miss.

MISS S  May I have them, please?

MR C  They *are* for you, are they?

MISS S  Yes. (*He hands them to her*) Thank you.

*She starts entering the information from the death certificate onto a form. Mr Crabtree watches very carefully.*

MISS S  Now then, sir, are you a relative of the deceased?

MR C  I am.

MISS S  Yes?

MR C  I am husband of the deceased.

MISS S  (*writing*) Thank you. And what was her full name?

MR C  Clara May Crabtree.

MISS S  (*writing*) What was her maiden name?

MR C  Clara May Radcliffe.

MISS S  And her date of birth?

MR C  I don't think she knew herself for definite ... She'd have been 82, all told, by Whitsun.

MISS S  81, then. (*Writing*) 'About 1894'. And *where* was she born?

MR C  Oh, a street or two from Peel Park, Accrington. I believe it's gone now.

MISS S  (*writing*) Accrington, Lancs. And what's *your* full name?

MR C  Henry Crabtree.

MISS S  (*writing*) And *your* date of birth?

MR C   Day after Boxing Day, 1896.

MISS S   (*writing*) 27.12.1896. And what is or was your occupation?

MR C   Weaver. Was. Six looms in my prime. Jacquard.

MISS S   (*writing*) Thank you. And where did your wife live, Mr Crabtree?

MR C   Her place of abode?

MISS S   Yes.

MR C   115, Latimer Street, end house. It's still *mine*. (*Pause*) The telly's on rental. (*Pause*) I shan't go bowling till after the funeral, for respect.

MISS S   (*sympathetically*) No. (*She writes one or two more details on the form.*) Do you have any Post Office Savings?

MR C   No.

MISS S   Any premium bonds?

MR C   No.

MISS S   No savings at all?

MR C   No.

MISS S   Have you any insurance you can claim?

MR C   Friendly Society.

MISS S   Good. (*She starts filling in the insurance form*)

MR C   Anyway, I've done my duty. Being next of kin. (*Pause*) She was a bit of a tinker at times, mind you. (*Pause*) At times? Most of the time. (*Pause*) She was a bit of a tinker for sixty years, to *my* knowledge. (*Pause*) Be quiet without her. (*Pause*) I caught the Number 26 to get here. Lower deck. Due to I don't smoke now. Gave it up ten years ago. At Clara's behest.

*Miss Shepherd begins handing him forms and pamphlets one by one.*

MISS S   Now, that's for the man from the Friendly Society. The green one's for the undertaker. And this one's for you to claim a death grant on the National Insurance. Just pop it in to your local Security Office. You know where that is, do you?

MR C   Oh, yes. I've been a good customer. (*Takes the documents*) Ta. I shan't go today. I'll save it for tomorrow.

*She smiles at him.*

MISS S   Thank you, Mr Crabtree.

MR C   Eh?

MISS S   Thank you.

MR C    Is that it?

MISS S    That's it.

*He sits, sadly puzzled and disappointed.*

MR C    I see. (*Pause*) You'd think there'd be more to it after all them years . . .

MISS S    We try and make it as . . .

MR C    Hang on! I forgot this! (*He hands her an aged, tattered document from his pension book*) Her birth certificate! It's got boot-blacking where the date should be . . .

MISS S    I don't need that, thanks.

MR C    Doesn't she have to give it in?

*Miss Shepherd shakes her head, smiling. Moved almost to tears.*

MR C    Gets to keep it, does she? I thought that now she'd finished with it . . . (*He puts it back in his pension book*) Anyway, it's been a day out. Met some interesting people. Conversed and that. In conversation.

*Unseen by Jenny or Miss Shepherd, busy sorting her documents, he unthinkingly take his chewing gum from his mouth and sticks it on the underside of the new desk.*
    *He rises, stand for a moment.*

MR C    Good line of business, really, isn't it? Yours? You do a brisk trade.

MISS S    (*smiling uncertainly*) Sorry?

MR C    Getting born, getting wed and passing over. I expect there's always a fair demand. Summer and winter.

MISS S    Yes. Yes, there is.

MR C    I'll say goodbye, then.

MISS S    'Bye, 'bye, Mr Crabtree.

MR C    (*to Jenny*) Good day, Miss.

JENNY    'Bye, now.

*He exits.*
    *Jenny continues working, singing quietly to herself.*
    *Miss Shepherd sits for a long moment, thoughtful, troubled.*
    *Jenny turns and grins at her.*

JENNY    Worth waiting for, then?

MISS S    Mmm?

JENNY    (*noddling towards the new desk*) Fabulous isn't it?

*Miss Shepherd surveys her desk, uneasy at a growing sense of anti-climax, of depression. A feeling of flatness she can't explain.*

MISS S  Lovely.

JENNY  (*laughing*) Hey! When you think of the old one!

MISS S  Yes.

JENNY  (*sighing contentedly*) Makes all the difference.

MISS S  Mmm?

JENNY  All the *difference*.

MISS S  Oh. Yes.

*Jenny returns to her work.*
*Miss Shepherd starts to attend to her papers and wriggles for a moment uncomfortably in her chair.*

MISS S  (*half to herself*) Damn chair. Before the ark this chair. Creaking and . . . needs slinging out altogether, really . . .

## 38  Barry's and Glenda's bedroom, early evening

*Glenda is drawing the covers over the baby in his crib. Barry, holding a nappy and bottle of talcum powder, is hovering beside her.*

GLENDA  Nighty, nighty, little Piggle-Poggle.

BARRY  See you soon, Daddy's Chumley-Bumley.

GLENDA  Have a nice sleepy, Little Pipsqueak.

## 39  Stan's bedsitter, early evening

*Stan, Liz, Mick and Mary lounging about, eating hamburgers from cardboard cartons, drinking from beer cans. The mood one of total relaxation. Liz is making a bit of a pig of herself with the food.*
*Mick notices, amused, and nudges Mary to look. She does.*

MARY  (*to Liz*) Hey. I thought your stomach was off?

LIZ  (*pleasantly, puzzled*) No?

MICK  You *said* it was.

LIZ  (*at peace*) You must be thinking of some *other* Mrs Turnbull.

## 40  Mr Crabtree's living room

*Mr Crabtree is sitting watching an early evening TV programme. He laughs at one of the jokes, and turns automatically, out of habit, to Clara's empty chair to share the joke with her. He realises, with almost no show of emotion at all, that she's not there. He turns back to the TV screen and continues laughing at the programme ... although his laughter is more subdued than a moment before.*

## 41 The car park, early evening

*Miss Shepherd passes through the gates, past Dan who is now polishing another car. Her sense of emptiness is now at its strongest.*

DAN Evening, Miss.

MISS S Evening, Dan.

DAN Well? Are you letting on?

MISS S (*puzzled*) Sorry?

DAN What was so special about it, then?

MISS S About what?

DAN Thursday. Nice day was it?

MISS S Oh ...fine. Bit like yesterday, really.

*She smiles and goes off to her car. Stay on Dan as he continues polishing.*

DAN (*to himself*) Tomorrow's *always* best.
(*Polishes away*) Nice lump of cod.
(*Pause: polishing away*) A few chips.
(*Pause: polishing away*) Plenty of vinegar ...

# Mr Ellis Versus the People

## The cast

Mr Ellis
Mr Martin
Miss Robinson (Petula)
Mrs Wendy Ellis
Mr Walmsley, *voter*
Plump woman, *voter*
Mrs Mobberley, *voter*
Mr Ridehalgh, *voter*
Mrs Ridehalgh, *voter*
Mr Crabtree, *voter*
Chinaman
Drunken voter
Bandaged man (*voter*)
Deirdre Skaife, *voter*
Terry Elliot, *voter*
Coughing voter
Male voter 1
Male voter 2
Male voter 3
Female voter 1
Female voter 2
Female voter 3
Dustman
Three loudspeaker voices

# Mr Ellis Versus the People

## 1 Main suburban streets (about 6.00 a.m.)

*The play opens with a sequence of shots of deserted streets, still fast asleep and silent.*

*Occasionally, a lone milkfloat is seen, or a postman.*

## 2 Suburban street A

*From one of the houses comes Mr Martin, a studious, sober-looking young man of about 20 or 21. He carries a crash helmet and briefcase. He stands for a moment on the step, deeply breathing in the morning air. He's being brisk, purposeful – and noble. It's rather a pity that there's no one around to be impressed by it.*

*Today, he feels, is the biggest day of his life. He walks round to the side of the house, and re-emerges, pushing his motor-scooter down to the gate. He gets on and chugs off down the empty, silent street.*

## 3 Suburban street B

*The camera slowly zooms in on the bedroom window of one of the houses. The curtains are still drawn. An alarm bell abruptly starts ringing. Then is quickly stopped.*

MRS E  Hey! Awkward!

MR E  Alright! I don't need your elbow in my ribs!

MRS E  It's twenty past six!

MR E  Will you stop digging me in the ribs, woman!

MRS E  What about tonight?

MR E  Oh, God . . . Here we go!

MRS E  What about tonight?

MR E  Wendy, I am not bandying words with you at twenty past six in the morning! Where's my socks?

### 4 Street C

*Mr Martin is seen chugging along nobly on his motor-scooter.*

### 5 Street D

*Petula (a young girl about 20), on her bike, is stopped by the traffic lights at red. She yawns, numbly. She tries to fight against her eyes closing ... and fails.*

*Cut to the lights changing from red to green and back again to red. She doesn't move. She's dozed off.*

### 6 Street B

*The bedroom window of the Ellis's house. Curtains still drawn.*

MRS E  You'll be late.

MR E  I've brought you up a cup of tea.

MRS E  What about tonight?

MR E  For crying out loud! Will you shut up about tonight!

*He draws the curtains open, then turns back to face into the room.*

MR E  Be careful with that cup!

*He dodges quickly to one side. A teacup hurtles against the window pane.*

### 7 The community hall

*Mr Martin wheels his scooter up to the entrance, passing directional signs reading 'Polling Station', and 'Way In', and posters announcing 'Parliamentary Bye-Election', 'Directions for the guidance of voters', and another showing which area is served by the Polling Station.*

*He rings the doorbell, importantly. No answer. He rings again, worriedly. No answer. He looks at his watch.*

MR M  Typical! Country with a major role in world affairs. No Presiding Officer. No key. (*He rings the bell again*) No answer.

*We hear a bicycle bell ring in reply. He turns to see Petula wheeling her bike towards him. On seeing him, Petula's sleepiness is almost – but not quite totally – replaced by adoration.*

PETULA  Morning, Mr Martin.

MR M  (*agitatedly*) Twenty to seven and it's locked! Have you read

Knight's Handbook for Presiding Officers and Polling Clerks?

PETULA  Well, I've . . .

MR M  Paragraph 15. Quote: 'A quarter of an hour is none too long for attending to the necessary details'. Unquote. (*Panicking*) A quarter of an hour! (*He rings the bell again*) And we've only twenty minutes!

*Petula stands sympathetically, at a loss. Mr Martin looks anxiously at his watch.*

PETULA  You don't think it could perhaps be under the mat?

MR M  (*pityingly*) Well, hardly, Miss Robinson. I mean it's hardly in keeping with the Representation of the People Act, 1949! *Or* it's amendment! (*Petula lifts up the doormat, and brings out a key, wrapped in a piece of notepaper*) Typical!

*He takes the key from her and unlocks the door. They wheel their scooter and bike into the foyer.*

## 8  The foyer

*They prop up the scooter and the bike against the wall. While Mr Martin is fussily seeing to his scooter, Petula reads the note the key was wrapped in.*

PETULA  'The heating is on. Will take time to warm up. When locking up, kindly replace key under mat, for security purposes. Have gone back to bed. T. Walley, caretaker'.

MR M  Absolutely typical.

*They go through into the hall.*

## 9  The hall

*There are three voting compartments (booths), two desks, three chairs, another chair near the booths with a battered ballot-box on it, another notice headed 'Directions for Guidance of Voters'. In each booth there is a notice stating that voters must vote for one candidate only, and a pinned-up ballot paper sample.*

    *Petula puts her bag on the desk, and wanders round the room, feeling the radiators.*

    *Mr Martin surveys the room, swelling with pride and awe.*

MR M  Can you feel it?

PETULA    Well, this one's boiling, that's freezing and that's making funny noises.

MR M    The *feeling*! The *atmosphere*. History, Tradition. Democracy, Miss Robinson. Government by the people for the people. The right of every single citizen, irrespective of . . . (*A thought suddenly strikes him. He wheels round on her, officiously*) Hang about!

PETULA    What?

MR M    What are *you* doing here anyway?

PETULA    (*guiltily*) I'm a polling clerk.

MR M    It's Miss Abbott, Libraries and Museums!

PETULA    (*more guiltily*) She's indisposed.

MR M    She was officially appointed on Monday with me and Mr Ellis! She made the declaration of secrecy!

PETULA    *I* did. Yesterday. When she was indisposed.

*He looks at her, suspiciously. She smiles at him, her eyes filled with adoration. He doesn't smile back. Hers fades. It hurts . . . but over the months she's got used to it. Petula starts taking from her bag her day's nourishment: apples, oranges, cheese, bananas, nuts, a carton of yoghourt, a box of wheatgerm, a box of vitamin E tablets, and a bottle of orange juice. Mr Martin watches her.*

MR M    A cup of coffee, Miss Robinson.

PETULA    I'll have my orange juice, thank you, Mr Martin. It's pure vita . . .

MR M    For me! A coffee for *me*!

PETULA    (*immediately stopping everything*) Oh, sorry! I've natural yoghourt if you prefer . . .

MR M    (*ignoring her*) You'll find the coffee things in the kitchen.

PETULA    It's full of goodness. It's equal to three hours sunshine in Torremolinos.

MR M    The kitchen's through the door with 'Kitchen' written on.

PETULA    Yes, Mr Martin.

*She gathers everything up, apart from some apples, oranges and bananas, and goes through to the kitchen. Mr Martin looks at his watch in growing concern.*

MR M    Quarter to. Nearly quarter to. Jesus.

*At a loss, he goes over to the ballot-box, tries it, hoping it's open. It isn't.*

MR M *(calling)* We can't open the poll without the Presiding Officer! That's the dilemma we're in . . .

PETULA You don't take horrible sugar, do you, Mr Martin?

MR M He should be here before any of us! There's a multitude of details to . . .

PETULA No horrible sugar, then?

MR M Four.

*He wanders towards the kitchen, ulcers growing by the second.*

## 10 The kitchen

*Petula is standing – fast asleep – with two cups at the ready, waiting for the kettle to boil. Mr Martin wanders, swallowing nervously. She hears him, and immediately jolts herself into action, clanking cups, milk bottle, whatever's at hand.*

MR M We're in a bit of a pickle, Miss Robinson . . .

*She smiles at him, tenderly.*

PETULA *(shyly)* I do have a *first* name, you know. Petula. Pet for short, but not for long. Corny joke . . .

MR M *(suddenly erupting)* God, it would happen. It's my first election, this!

PETULA *(interpreting this as a wonderful new bond between them)* Me too.

MR M I was hoping it'd all go really . . . I mean, organisation-wise, you'd think it'd . . . I was up at five o'clock this morning, revising my handbook! I've been learning it for a fortnight! My mother's been testing me on it every . . .

PETULA *(fighting back sleep)* Does your head feel a long way from your body?

MR M *(abstractly)* What?

PETULA My face won't wake up. It keeps doing what it wants. *(He takes his watch off and holds it to his ear. Listens. Shakes it again. She looks at him and smiles shyly)* Anyway . . . At last.

MR M *(preoccupied)* Mmm?

PETULA At last.

MR M What at last?

PETULA Us. Working together. In the same department. Well, same place. For a day anyway. At last.

MR M *(ignoring her)* I think we're definitely in a bit of a pickle situation, Miss Robinson. I think we're supposed to ring the

Town Hall. I think it's obligatory. (*He gets his handbook out of his pocket and checks*) It *is* obligatory. We're obliged to ring the Returning Officer at the Town Hall. Oh, hell. (*He sighs, looks at his watch, panics even more*) Oh, hell!!

*Quite a long silence.*

PETULA  It's true about a watched kettle, isn't it?

MR M  We'd better ring the Returning Officer. It's very nearly going on for nearly ten to. I think what we'd better do is ring the Returning Officer. (*He looks at her suspiciously*) What exactly's wrong with Miss Abbott, Libraries and Museums?

PETULA  (*guiltily*) She's indisposed.

MR M  How exactly?

PETULA  I think she's probably got a bug.

MR M  Uh, uh. Sudden, was it? Or pre-arranged?

PETULA  (*even more guiltily*) How do you mean – pre-arranged? I don't know how you mean! Why should it be pre-arranged?

MR M  *You* tell *me*.

PETULA  (*evasively*) Do you think we'd better ring the Returning Officer?

*Mr Martin looks at his watch.*

MR M  (*scared*) Do *you*?

PETULA  Oh, hell! I forgot to switch it on!

*She switches the kettle on.*


## 11 The hall

*Mr Ellis enters.*

MR E  (*calling*) Shop!

*He puts his briefcase down on the table. Mr Martin dashes out of the kitchen, bathed in relief.*

MR M  Morning, Mr Ellis. Have you been inadvertently delayed?

MR E  Mmm?

MR M  I thought perhaps you'd been delayed inadvertently.

MR E  (*blankly*) No?

MR M  Oh. It's just that I was contemplating ringing the Town Hall. It'll soon be nearly going on for nearly five to . . .

MR E  (*calmly, without looking at his watch*) It's ten to. I *time* it to arrive ten to. Every election day the same.

154

*As he speaks, he sits down and takes two pipes, matches, tobacco and a pair of slippers from his briefcase. He changes into the slippers as he talks. As he does so, we get a glimpse of his pyjamas underneath his trousers.*

MR E  Up at twenty past six. Four minutes row with *Mrs* Ellis. Twelve minutes to wash, dress and spill my cornflakes. Another three minutes rowing with Mrs Ellis, repeating everything I said the first time. Six minutes getting the car started, and five minutes drive. Ten to. Right?

*Mr Martin checks his watch.*

MR M  Yes.

MR E  Good. (*Glances towards the polling compartments*) Notices in each compartment, yes?

MR M  Yes.

MR E  Right. Ballot box.

*Mr Martin goes to collect it from its chair.*

MR M  (*calling towards the kitchen*) Another coffee, please, Miss Robinson!

MR E  Tea.

MR M  (*calling*) Tea! (*To Mr Ellis*) Sugar?

MR E  Arsenic'll do.

MR M  (*calling*) No sugar!

MR E  Who the hell's Miss Robinson, then?

MR M  (*bringing him the ballot box*) Acting polling clerk.

MR E  It's Miss Abbott, Libraries and Museums.

MR M  It's Miss Robinson now. Parks and Gardens.

*Mr Ellis takes the ballot box.*

MR E  Right. Key. (*He starts feeling in his pockets*) Key. Key. (*He continues feeling and patting pockets. Mr Martin begins to panic again. He looks at his watch. Mr Ellis finally finds the key in one of his pockets*) Ah.

*Mr Martin relaxes again. Mr Ellis tries to open the box. The key sticks.*

MR E  Moses brought the tablets down Mount Sinai in these, you know. And they were rusted to hell *then*. You'd think computers had never been invented, wouldn't you?

MR M  (*heart sinking*) Is something broken?

MR E  (*calmly*) Just my spirit, laddie, that's all. (*Mr Martin looks at his watch. Mr Ellis notices)* It's not a race, Mr Martin. A trial by ordeal, yes. An endurance test, OK.

MR M  Pardon?

MR E  Please stop looking at your watch. We're here for another fifteen hours yet. It'll still be there. Ticking away. Like clockwork . . .

*He finally opens the box and starts to empty documents from it. Mr Martin watches him, concerned.*

MR M  Um . . .

MR E  *(stopping to look at him)* What now?

MR M  Aren't we supposed to check, Mr Ellis?

MR E  *(wearily)* Check what, Mr Martin?

MR M  The contents.

*Mr Ellis looks at him . . . and sighs.*

MR E  Your first election, right?

MR M  Well . . . virtually.

MR E  Why – how many have you done before?

MR M  None.

MR E  I've done the lot since 1945. I've seen them all. The great and the near great. Attlee, Churchill, Eden, Macmillan, Home, Wilson, Heath and Mrs Ellis. The contents will be correct. They always are.

MR M  I believe the handbook more or less advises they should be checked.

MR E  Does it now?

MR M  I believe so.

*He starts getting the handbook from his pocket.*

MR E  *(wearily)* Don't bother.

*Mr Martin takes the list of contents from the ballot box, and calls out each item in turn, like a surgeon at the operating table. Mr Ellis, fed up, verifies each in turn, taking them from the box and placing them on the table.*

MR M  Electoral register.

MR E  Electoral register.

MR M  Absent voters list.

MR E  Absent voters list.

MR M  Proxy voters.

MR E  Proxy voters.

MR M  Proxies entitled to vote by post.

MR E  Proxies entitled to vote by post.

MR M  Ballot papers.

MR E  Ballot papers.

MR M  Stamping instrument.

MR E  Stamping instrument.

MR M  (*calling towards kitchen*) We're still patiently waiting for tea and coffee, Miss Robinson!

## 12 The kitchen

*Petula, once again asleep, is standing before the kettle and cups. She jumps awake.*

PETULA  Yes! Coming!

*She picks up the three mugs and exits.*

## 13 The hall

*Mr Martin and Mr Ellis, as before. Petula wanders in during the following dialogue.*

MR M  Ballot paper account form.

MR E  Ballot paper account form.

MR M  Tendered votes.

MR E  Tendered votes.

MR M  Statement of votes marked by Presiding Officer.

MR E  Statement.

*He watches Petula as she puts their two mugs down on the desk.*

PETULA  Coffee, four sugars, tea, no sugar. (*To Mr Ellis*) Good morning.

MR E  Morning. I'm Mr Ellis.

MR M  Presiding Officer. This is Miss Robinson. Parks and Gardens.

PETULA  How do you do.

MR E  And what happened to Miss Abbott, then?

PETULA  She's indisposed. (*Guilty glance at Mr Martin*)

MR E  I'm surprised she's not crippled for life. Platform heels she wears ...

PETULA  (*eager to end further discussion of Miss Abbott's indisposition*) Yes. I'll just give this to the bobby.

*She starts for the door, with the mug.*

MR M (*resuming his list*) Pencils!

MR E Mmm? (*Realises he's continuing*) Oh, pencils.

MR M Ink, pens, paper, envelopes.

MR E Yes.

MR M Large envelopes.

MR E Right. And sealing wax and tape.

MR M Correct.

MR E Geronimo. (*The box is now empty*) Happy now?

MR M Yes, thanks.

MR E Good. (*He starts to sip his tea*)

MR M (*troubled*) Um . . .

*Mr Ellis lowers his mug of tea, wearily.*

MR E You're not, then?

MR M Aren't you supposed to show – quote – 'the empty box to such persons, if any, as are present in the station, so that they can see it's empty' – unquote?

MR E That'll be your handbook again, will it?

MR M Paragraph 28.

*Mr Ellis angles the box so that Mr Martin can see inside.*

MR E Well?

MR M Empty.

MR E Super.

*He locks the box and starts applying his seal.*

MR E Lock the door while you're there, love. (*She does so*) And did you bring your appointment form?

PETULA Yes.

*She goes to her huge bag to rummage inside.*

MR M You're obliged to show it to the Presiding Officer.

PETULA Yes, I am doing . . .

MR M (*with a sideways glance to Mr Ellis to see if he's impressed*) And did you make the statutory declaration of secrecy, Miss Robinson?

PETULA Pardon?

MR M To the Returning Officer at the Town Hall.

PETULA Yesterday. I told you.

MR M (*to Mr Ellis*) That's alright then.

MR E I bet *you* know it by heart, don't you?

MR M   (*briskly*) 'I solemnly promise and declare that I will not do anything forbidden by sub-sections 1, 2, 3 and 6 of Section 53 of the Representation of the People Act, 1949, which have been read to me'.

MR E   Ten out of ten. Go and put the pencils in the booths.

*Mr Martin, very slightly put out, obeys. Petula gives Mr Ellis her appointment card.*

PETULA   My appointment card, Mr Ellis.

MR E   Good girl, Miss Robinson. (*He glances towards the booths, where Mr Martin is distributing the pencils*) It's going to be a long day . . . with William Pitt the Younger over there . . .

PETULA   (*contentedly*) Yes. Isn't it?


## 14  The hall

*Everything is now ready for the opening of the poll. Mr Ellis sits between Mr Martin and Petula at the desk. The ballot box is on its chair between the desk and the booths. Mr Ellis distributes papers and documents along the desk.*

MR E   Special lists. Absent voters. Proxies. Postal proxies. Register. (*Glancing at ballot box*) Biscuit tin visible from desk? Right.

*They sit quietly sipping their tea, coffee and orange juice.*

MR E   OK, Mr Martin, *now* you can look at your watch. (*Mr Martin does so*) What's it got to say for itself?

MR M   One minute fifteen seconds to seven.

MR E   (*winks*) Point taken?

MR M   (*grinning*) Yes.

MR E   Good.

*He settles back with his tea. After all the pace of the previous scenes, all is at last silent and peaceful. They sip their drinks.*

MR E   Best part of the day, this. Savour every second. In a couple of hours you'll look back on it as the happiest time of your life.

*Petula smiles lovingly – albeit sleepily – at Mr Martin. He ignores her, and takes out his handbook for one last anxious revision. Petula begins to nod off again. The peace is abruptly shattered by the 'phone ringing harshly in the Committee Room. Mr Martin jumps, edgily.*

MR E   (*calmly*) That'll be my wife. Ignore it.

MR M  What if it isn't?

MR E  It will be.

MR M  It could be the Returning Officer!

MR E  The Returning Officer isn't trying to drive me barmy.

PETULA  I'll go and see.

> *She gets up and starts for the committee room. Mr Ellis smiles at Mr Martin.*

MR E  Nervous?

MR M  Nervous? No, not *nervous*. Not at all. (*Nervously*) It's a terrific responsibility, isn't it?

MR E  You might be a Presiding Officer one day. How's that grab you?

MR M  Me? (*Laughs diffidently, then humbly*) Well, if the mantle of greatness happens to be thrust upon me ...

MR E  Then what? Returning Officer, perhaps ...

MR M  Well, local government is certainly a terrific challenge ...

MR E  Then, in the fulness of time, who knows? Whitehall?

MR M  Possibly. I'm only a relative beginner, really ...

## 15 The committee room

> *Petula picks up the 'phone.*

PETULA  Polling Station Number Three – no, sorry – Four, good morning. (*Pause*) Hang on. (*Calling*) It *is* your wife, Mr Ellis.

## 16 The hall

> *Mr Ellis and Mr Martin at the desk.*

MR E  If she so much as mentions the word 'tonight', tell her you're reporting her to the GPO for obscene 'phone calls. (*Resumes his conversation with Mr Martin*) Then what? Member of Parliament? Fancy being an MP?

MR M  Well, it would certainly be a terrific challenge ...

MR E  Prime Minister? Am I sharing a teaspoon with a future Prime Minister?

MR M  (*soberly*) I think it's a bit early to say yet, to be honest. I daresay I've a lot to learn ... I'd be as good as some of them, I daresay ...

MR E  We get the government we deserve, Mr Martin.

*Petula returns to the desk.*

PETULA  I think she heard you. She hung up.

MR E  That's a good sign. (*Looks at his watch*) Well ... eight seconds to go. (*He smiles at their earnest faces*) Good luck, Mr Martin.

MR M  (*stiffening, tensely*) Thank you.

MR E  Good luck, Miss Robinson.

PETULA  Thank you. You, too.

MR E  Say farewell for ever to your youthful innocence. Open the door, Miss Robinson. (*She goes over to the main door*) (*To Mr Martin*) And something else you'll learn before the day's out – governments get the *electorate* they deserve. Poor sods. (*A deep breath, then to Petula*) OK, love, wheel them in.

*The Town Hall clock begins to chime seven o'clock in the distance. Mr Martin stiffens.*

MR E  Ask not for whom the bell tolls, Mr Martin. You'll see.

*With a shaking yawn, Petula lifts the catch and opens the door.*

## 17  The hall

*Mr Ellis, Mr Martin and Petula extremely busily at work.*

*Mr Martin and Petula seated at the desk, Mr Ellis hovering behind them, leaning over to stamp ballot papers, as each voter registers.*

*Two voters are marking their papers in the booths, a third is putting his folded ballot paper into the box. A fourth is just leaving the desk en route to the vacant booth, a fifth is at the desk registering as a sixth enters and a seventh leaves.*

*There is constant movement throughout. The Presiding Officer wouldn't allow over-crowding or queuing.*

*All voters are one of two things – either nervous and ill-at-ease, not knowing quite what to do or where to go – or rude, self-important and pompous toward the Presiding Officer and his Polling Clerks. We see these characteristics, except where indicated, throughout.*

*The voter at the desk is Mr Walmsley.*

MR M  Do you have your polling card, please.

MR W  Well, would you Christmas-Eve it!! I knew I'd forgot *something*!

MR M  That's all you had to remember.

MR W  Yes, I know.

MR M  Well, could I have your name and address, please?

*From outside we hear a voice calling through the loudspeaker of a car.*

LOUDSP 1　Today is polling day. Today is polling day. Vote for the party that cares. Vote Labour.

*Another voice on a loudspeaker is heard from another car.*

LOUDSP 2　Today is polling day. Vote Liberal – the party that –
LOUDSP 1　Vote Labour. Today is polling day –
LOUDSP 2　Change to Liberal. Vote Liberal today –
MR E　(*to Petula*) Get the constable to clear Simon and Garfunkel away, will you? They know they're not allowed near here.

*She gets up and goes.*

MR W　You know what I've done, don't you? Brought my laundry list, and left my polling card on the mantelpiece . . .
MR M　That's alright, if I can just have your . . .
MR W　No, hang on! (*He searches through his wallet*) I've left them *both* on the mantelpiece . . . Gordon Walmsley, 18 Wellington Street.

*Mr Martin searches his register, ticks off the name, Mr Ellis stamps the next ballot paper, and gives it to Mr Martin who hands it to Mr* `Wamsley.

MR M　Thank you.
MR W　You're welcome.

*He starts to exit.*

MR M　Aren't you going to vote?
MR W　(*turning*) Eh? (*Realises what he's doing*) Oh, yes. (*He turns back and goes to a booth to vote*)


## 18 The hall (some time later)

*Mr Ellis, Mr Martin and Petula, amid more voters, working away non–stop.*

*A plump woman wearing a Labour rosette is at the desk.*

PETULA　Have you got your polling card, please?
PLUMP WO　Have you got a toilet?
PETULA　Pardon?
PLUMP WO　Have you got a . . . Is there such a thing as a . . . I'm looking for . . .

MR E *(pointing to the changing room door)* Through there, love.
PLUMP WO Thank you.

*She starts to go.*

MR E You'll take your rosette off first, won't you, love?
PLUMP WO *(stopping)* Take my what off?
MR E *(signals a rosette on his lapel and points to hers)* Not allowed.
PLUMP WO I'm only going to the toilet.
MR E Sorry. Against the rules.
PETULA *(as the plump woman begins to wrestle with her rosette)* Would you like your ballot paper now, or after you've ...
PLUMP WO *(starting off again)* After.

*She goes off to the changing room, struggling with her rosette.*

### 19 The hall (some time later)

*Mr Ellis, Mr Martin and Petula still working away with the next influx of voters.*
 *Mrs Mobberley, in her 60s, approaches the desk.*

MRS M Conservative.
MR M What??
MRS M Conservative, please. Thank you.

*She starts to go out again.*

MR E A moment, madam, please. *(She stops)* Do you have your polling card?
MRS M My who?
MR E It should have come in the post.
MRS M I've never had one. There's all sorts of stuff I never get.
MR E No ... well, can you tell me your name and address, please?
MRS M I've had a leaflet about learning Kung-Fu.
MR M Can I have your name and address, please.
MRS M I thought it was supposed to be secret?
MR M Not your name and address. Only your *vote*.
MRS M Conservative.
MR M *(agitated)* You mustn't tell us. That's the whole object of the ballot! We have to give you a ballot-paper, then you go across there and ...
MRS M Just because you lot's nowt better to do, it doesn't mean to say *I* haven't ... Sat here polishing your breeches behinds all day ... You drive us silly to come and vote and then

when we do . . . (*She simmers down, and snaps her name out*) Mrs Mobberley, 47 Charlotte Street.

MR M  (*relieved*) Thank you, madam,

MRS M  Conservative.


### 20  The hall

*A moment's respite at the desk – the later influx of voters are now depositing their ballot papers and leaving.*

*Mr Martin sighs, sleepily. Mr Ellis lights his pipe and relaxes. Petula takes an apple from her bag.*

PETULA  Can I tempt you to an apple, Mr Martin?

MR M  No thanks.

PETULA  It's a Golden Delicious.

MR M  No, honestly.

*Petula takes a bite of her apple, glances at Mr Ellis, then double-takes. He appears to be arguing with himself. He notices her looking.*

MR E  Sorry . . . I was just having a row with the wife about tonight. I was *winning* an' all. Had her snookered all ends up. Doesn't happen often.

PETULA  What about tonight?

MR E  Don't *you* start.

*Cut to a voter – Mr Crabtree – in one of the booths. He turns and calls to them.*

MR C  Excuse me! Are you there?

MR E  Hello?

MR C  I've voted for the wrong one.

MR E  Sorry?

MR C  I've put it in the wrong square.

MR E  Bring me the ballot paper, sir. I'll give you another.

*Mr Crabtree goes to the desk and gives Mr Ellis his spoiled paper.*

MR C  It's only nerves.

MR E  Easily done.

MR C  Like taking your exams in a way, isn't it?

MR E  Well . . . not really.

*During the above four lines, Mr Ellis has taken the spoiled vote, made a note on his President Officer's statement and stamped another ballot paper for him.*

MR C   (*taking it*) Cheers. (*He returns to the booth*)

MR E   (*wearily*) Right ... Stretch my legs a minute before the acrobats come on.

*He starts off on a little stroll round the hall. After a moment or two we see him resume his imaginary argument with his wife.*

    *Petula eats her apple. Mr Martin breathes deeply to try and keep awake. She smiles fondly at him. He ignores her.*

PETULA   You never seem to pop into our department much these days. Not since Clifford was transferred to Engineers and Surveyors ...

MR M   Mmm? No. No, well, he's in the same backgammon club as me, you see.

PETULA   Yes, so he said. He reckoned you were sensational at backgammon. Out on your own.

MR M   Yeah, I'm not bad.

PETULA   It must be terrifically interesting. (*No reaction from Mr Martin*) I'd love to learn. (*Still no reaction*) You know, if anyone would be kind enough to teach me ...

MR M   Have a word with Clifford.

PETULA   (*squashed*) Oh. Yes. (*Head aching*) Good idea.

*Cut to Mr Crabtree in his booth.*

MR C   Excuse me! Are you there? (*All three look at him*) I've only done it again, haven't I?

MR E   I'll give you another.

*Wearily he makes his way back to the desk. Mr Crabtree joins him. They go through the same procedure as earlier.*

MR C   (*nervous, embarrassed*) I bet that's a record, isn't it? Mucking up two.

MR E   Oh, you'd be surprised.

MR C   Must drive you potty.

MR E   We get used to it.

MR C   Get all of a dither, somehow, don't you? Just as you're marking your vote. Funny, really ...

MR E   (*sighing*) Yes, well, we like a good laugh ...

*Mr Crabtree returns to the booth with his new ballot paper. Mr Ellis resumes his stroll round. Petula racks her brains to contrive another advance to Mr Martin.*

PETULA  (*not quite as nonchalantly as she hopes*) I don't think you *came* to the NALGO dance, did you. I don't think . . .?

MR M  No.

PETULA  No, I didn't think you did. I think Sandra Tattersall was keeping her fingers crossed you would. I think she's possibly a bit keen on you, Sandra Tattersall . . .

MR M  (*sighing, impatiently*) Miss Robinson . . .

PETULA  (*heart somersaulting*) 'Petula' . . .

MR M  I happen to subscribe to the theory there are more important things in life than dancing with Sandra Tattersall.

PETULA  Oh, granted.

MR M  Do you have your polling card, please?

VOTER  (*Handing him the card*) Sorry about the state it's in. The baby was eating it.

*Mr Martin checks the register. Petula sits, eating her heart out.*

MR M  (*to the voter*) Henry St John Tarquin Skidmore?

VOTER  Correct.

*Mr Martin stamps a ballot paper and gives it to him. He goes off to a booth.*

PETULA  I think perhaps Sandra Tattersall's point was that some boys seem to quite *like* having a girlfriend. I don't mean *serious* or anything – heaven forbid! – not steady – just sort of . . .

MR M  Yes, well, I've a career to carve out for myself, haven't I? A future.

PETULA  Yes. Quite right, too. (*Pause. One last try*) I mean it doesn't have to be Sandra Tattersall . . .

MR M  What doesn't?

PETULA  Nothing. I was agreeing.

MR C  (*in his booth*) Oh, bloody ding-dong!!

*They all look at him.*

MR E  (*deadpan*) You've done it again.

MR C  No, I've broken the point off the pencil.

MR E  (*indicating she gives him a pencil*) Miss Robinson.

MR C  Pressing too hard, I should imagine. In all probability . . .

*Mr Ellis turns away, softly singing to himself 'Oh, God, our help in ages past' for strength and comfort.*

*A middle-aged woman enters and approaches Petula and Mr Martin at the desk. It's Mr Ellis's wife, Wendy.*

PETULA  Do you have your polling card, please?

MRS E  1839. Mrs Wendy Ellis.

*Mr Ellis swivels round on hearing the name. He sees her. His heart sinks.*

MR E  Hello, love.

MRS E  (*to Petula*) 22 Nantwich Lane.

*Petula and Mr Martin look at Mr Ellis and exchange a fractional glance of apprehension.*
*Mr Ellis, once more behind the desk, hands Wendy a ballot paper.*

MRS E  Thank you.

*She starts towards one of the booths. Mr Ellis catches up with her. They talk in loud whispers.*

MR E  You've come for a row, haven't you? I can tell by your handbag. I'm not bandying words with you during office hours . . .

MRS E  I've come to cast my vote, if you don't mind.

MR E  Now listen, Wendy. Any misconduct and I'm reluctantly compelled to have you ejected by the Duty Constable – Knights Handbook for Presiding Officers and Clerks.

MR M  (*to Petula*) Paragraph 77.

*She steps into the booth to mark her vote. He follows her.*

MRS E  I was under the impression this was supposed to be private.

*He moves back towards the desk, watching her, warily. She marks her ballot paper. Mr Ellis, Mr Martin and Petula wait tensely, apprehensively for the sudden eruption.*
*Mrs Ellis drops her folded ballot paper into the box.*
*Mr Ellis looks for a means of escaping from the imminent confrontation. He finds one.*

MR E  Carry on as though I weren't here.

*He exits through the door marked 'Changing Rooms and Toilets'.*
*Wendy starts for the kitchen, then stops.*

MRS E  (*To Petula and Mr Martin*) Fancy a cup of tea?

PETULA  Um . . . er . . . I'd quite like some orange juice, Mrs Ellis, thank you. I have a bottle in the kitchen.

MRS E  Young man?

MR M  (*anxiously*) Actually Mrs Ellis, with all due respect, you're actually forbidden to remain on the premises after you've . . .

MRS E  Just one orange juice and one cup of tea, then.

*She continues towards the kitchen. Mr Martin gets up, agitatedly.*

MR M  I'm sorry, Mrs Ellis! But, by law, you're . . .

MRS E  Don't be sorry, son. It'll be less washing-up.

*She exits into the kitchen.*
    *Mr Martin stares after her, the morning's frustrations and exasperating boiling up. They finally explode.*

MR M  We're supposed to be the most politically sophisticated society in the world! Alastair Burnet's always saying so! Robert Mackenzie nearly wets himself saying so! All they've to do is identify themselves, make a bloody cross on a piece of bloody paper, stick it in a bloody box and go home! And they can't! Every single one of them's a bloody . . .

PETULA  Don't swear, Mr Martin. I haven't come to expect it from you . . .

MR M  (*murderously*) There are three people allowed in this polling station! Me, you and Mr Ellis! It's not a chimpanzees' bloody tea-party!!

PETULA  No.

*Worriedly, absently, she takes a banana from her bag and starts to peel it.*

PETULA  Shall I go and tell her?

MR M  *I'll* go and tell her!

PETULA  No, you get Mr Ellis back out. Two of you have to be on duty . . .

MR M  I'll bloody tell her alright!!

*He charges off to the kitchen.*
    *A man enters smoking a cigarette and coughing his heart out.*

PETULA  Do you have your polling card, please?

*He coughs some reply.*

## 21 The kitchen

*Wendy is preparing a cup of tea and glass of orange juice. Mr Martin bursts in.*

MR M  Mrs Ellis! According to the second schedule of the Representation of the People Act, 19 . . .

MRS E  (*gently while working*) Do you know Mr Bainbridge?

MR M  The Mayor? Well, we've met. In the course of duty. In his official capacity as . . .

MRS E  (*quietly, matter-of-fact*) Every election right, the Mayor invites the Presiding Officers and their wives to the Town Hall. (*Mr Martin impatiently gets out his handbook*) After the count they have drinks in the Mayor's Parlour. It's Mr Bainbridge this year.

MR M  (*finding the relevant page*) Mrs Ellis, if you'd just care to glance at . . .

MRS E  I believe they have little sausages on sticks and kipper pâté and mushroom vol-au-vents and everything. The Lady Mayoress is spending all day preparing it. She's a wonderful cook . . . I believe her grandmother was half-French . . .

MR M  Mrs Ellis . . .

MRS E  It's the Mayor's way of saying thank you for their efforts. The wives wear evening dress. The men don't, of course; they've been in the polling stations for fifteen hours. But everyone laughs and talks and arranges Tupperware parties. It's the most glittering occasion in the social calendar.

*A pause.*
   *Mr Martin has simmered down. He's become more than a little interested.*

MRS E  (*matter-of-factly*) And we've never been to *one*. Every election night since 1945, my husband crawls home about half-past-ten with a bag of fish and chips and goes to bed. (*Pause*) He doesn't even stay up to watch the swingometer.

*A silence.*
   *Wendy gives Mr Martin the cup of tea.*

MRS E  That's for Mr Ellis. He's devoted his life to breaking the world tea-drinking record.

MR M  (*abashed*) I thought it was for *you* . . .

MRS E  (*handing him the glass of orange juice*) And that's for the young lady. Is she your girlfriend?

MR M   No, no.

MRS E   She's probably playing hard to get. You must be showing her too *much* consideration. Of course, you're not married to her yet.

*She exits to the hall.*

## 22   The hall

*Mrs Ellis emerges from the kitchen and crosses towards the main door. Petula has just finished her banana and started on a bag of nuts. One or two more voters in evidence.*

MRS E   'Bye, 'bye, Miss. Tell Mr Ellis I've taken the car to go shopping. He can bring his chips back on the bus.

*She exits. Mr Martin emerges from the kitchen with the tea and orange juice. He appears sober and thoughtful. He puts the drinks on the desk, Petula sees the orange juice: it's the nicest thing he's ever done for her.*

PETULA   Oh, *thank you*, Mr Martin! That's very considerate.

MR M   Mmm? (*Realises what she's on about*) Oh. *She* poured it out.

PETULA   Still. You brought it. (*She takes a sip by way of appreciation. She looks at his thoughtful face*) Don't feel bad. It's one of the burdens of responsibility and leadership. You had to sling her out. (*Smiles hero-worship*) And you did.

MR M   (*thoughtfully: a little excitedly*) Did you know they have a sort of think-tank at the Mayor's Parlour tonight? Intriguing that, isn't it? All the senior staff there ... conversing, analysing ... having fairly perceptive discussions, I should imagine ...

*Mr Ellis strolls out of the changing room, in his shirt sleeves, towelling his wet hair. He looks round calmly.*

MR E   Mrs Ellis gone then ... cue for applause?

PETULA   Yes. Just. Have you been having a bath?

MR E   Shower. Interesting footballers they must have changing in there of a Saturday. I found two jars of make-up remover pads and a hairnet ...

MR M   Mrs Ellis left that for you. (*Indicating cup of tea*)

MR E   Did she now? Crafty monkey. Have you thought about lunch, you two?

MR M  Mmm? (*Looks at his watch*)

MR E  Think about it.

MR M  I'll make myself a coffee. The kettle's already ...

PETULA  (*half raising from her chair*) Shall *I* do it for you?

> *Mr Martin continues to the kitchen and exits.*
> *Petula sits down again, sighing.*

MR E  You must have your lunch soon, love. You'll need every ounce of energy you've got for tonight.

PETULA  (*eating her nuts*) I'm not all that hungry, actually.

> *He looks at her.*

MR E  Anything wrong? Apart from life?

PETULA  Nothing.

MR E  Good.

PETULA  (*tears imminent*) I just don't know how to get *through* to him! Everything I do, he just ... He doesn't even seem to know I ... I mean he's so ... Well, I suppose *all* great men are, underneath. For all we know, *Mrs* Pitt the Younger was probably on *Librium* ...

MR E  Yes. (*Pause*) I'll go and warm my dinner plate. I'm having mine in there. (*Nods towards kitchen*) Presiding Officer's privilege.

> *Mr Martin comes out of the kitchen, with his mug of steaming coffee.*
> *Mr Ellis makes his way to the kitchen. He stops and looks thoughtfully at them both.*

MR E  Play nice while I'm away. There'll be another mad rush in about twenty minutes.

> *He exits to the kitchen.*
> *Mr Martin starts taking sandwiches from his briefcase.*

PETULA  (*re the coffee*) I'd have made it for you ...

MR M  (*ignoring her*) Imagine, though. All the best brains of the Town Hall. All there together. Wheeler-dealing. Jockeying for position. Hell, it'd be worth getting invited to, that. One day. Corridors of power. The right word in the right ear. I mean, he's a *kingmaker* is Mr Bainbridge. There's no telling where ...

PETULA  (*bursting*) Mr Martin! Don't you ever, *ever* think about anything apart from ... I mean ...

*She breaks off on seeing Mr Martin staring at an attractive young girl (Deirdre Skaife) who's just entered.*

MR M    (*almost to himself*) I wouldn't mind jockeying for position with *that* for an hour or two ... (*She looks at him incredulously, then back at the girl. Deirdre approaches the desk*) (*Meaningful smile*) May I help you, Miss? Or is it Mrs?

DEIRDRE   (*well-practised coy smile*) Oh, just Miss. (*She gives him her polling card*) Miss Deirdre Skaife.

MR M    (*smiling back*) Nice name.

DEIRDRE   Thank you.

MR M    (*checking her card against the register*) 17 Meadow Court, Manchester Road?

DEIRDRE   That's right.

MR M    The block of flats.

DEIRDRE   Right again.

MR M    (*looks at list. Smiles at her again*) No other voters at number 17?

DEIDRE   No one else *lives* there. Apart from Streaker. Half-Siamese, half-Persian, and stays out all night.

*Petula has meanwhile coldly stamped the ballot paper and thrust it at her.*

DEIRDRE   Ta.

*She goes off to the booth to vote. Mr Martin watches her admiringly. Petula sits staring ahead, tensely, fighting back the tears.*

MR M    He once called me by name, actually, did Mr Bainbridge. Outside the Treasurer's Office. He ...

*A tough-looking young lad, in oil-stained overalls, enters. He's unshaven and dirty-faced. A bit of rough. This is Terry Elliot.*

PETULA   (*smiling seductively*) Hi, there.

TERRY    (*slightly puzzled at her warmth*) How do.

PETULA   (*as though she was asking him to take his clothes off*) Do you have your polling card, please?

TERRY    (*smiling back*) Sorry. I forgot.

PETULA   (*smiling*) No hassle. Would you mind giving me your name, then, please?

TERRY    Not at all darling. Terry Elliott. Well, Terence, really. 158 Sankey Road.

*Petula takes the register from in front of Mr Martin.*

PETULA   Excuse me (*She checks Terry's name in the list, smiles at him*) Thank you. Terence.

TERRY   (*grinning*) Don't thank me. I haven't done nowt. Yet.

PETULA   (*smiling coyly*) Asked for that, didn't I?

*She stamps his ballot paper and gives it to him. He winks at her and goes off to the booth. Mr Martin has watched the whole performance with incredulity, disgust . . . and envy.*

MR M   Yes. You *did* rather.

*Deirdre, having deposited her ballot paper, is now leaving.*

DEIRDRE   (*to Mr Martin*) 'Bye, then.

*Mr Martin is too busy looking at Petula, waiting probably for some sort of apology, to even notice.*
   *Deirdre, slightly puzzled, exits.*

MR M   Miss Robinson? (*She ignores him*) I said 'Yes, you did rather', Miss Robinson. Ask for it . . .

*A Chinaman, wearing a lounge suit and carrying a small carrier-bag, has entered and is making his way to the desk.*

PETULA   Do you have your polling card, please?

CHINAMAN   (*not understanding*) Please?

PETULA   Your polling card.

*Terry is now leaving the hall. He winks at Petula as he goes. She gives him a smile and small wave.*

MR M   Can we have your name or number, then, please.

CHINAMAN   Number?

PETULA   Yes, please.

CHINAMAN   I think . . . 7, 23 and 41.

*They look at him blankly.*

MR M   Just *one* number.

CHINAMAN   No, no. 7, 23, 41. Spare ribs, sweet and sour prawns and pancake roll. (*They stare at him*) Mr Ellis. (*They still don't understand*) Ready order.

PETULA   Oh! Mr Ellis's lunch?

CHINAMAN   (*smiling and nodding*) Yes, please.

PETULA   Through there, then.

CHINAMAN   Please.

*He goes to the kitchen, knocks and enters. A silence. Mr Martin sips his coffee, and munches a sandwich; Petula starts on a carton of yoghourt from her bag.*

MR M   OK?

PETULA   What?

MR M   You. OK. Everything OK?

PETULA   (*coolly*) Never better, thanks.

MR M   Good. (*A lengthy pause. Petula busy ignoring him*) Fair enough, we may have had one or two minor problems, but they happen in the best regulated polling stations ... Everything's under control, really. The old ballot box slowly filling. The voice of the nation quietly making itself heard. Organisation, you see. Efficiency, concentration on the job in hand ... You see, if we get an 80 per cent poll and ... (*He reaches for the register. In so doing he knocks his cup of hot coffee all over it*) Oh, my God!

*Petula screams. They both leap to their feet – trying to rescue the register, tearing at it, as coffee flows all over its pages.*

MR M   Oh, my God!!

PETULA   (*hysterically, as she tries to wipe the pages*) They're sodden. They're stuck together. You can't see who's voted and who ... Or the names! The whole poll! It's ruined!

MR M   Oh, my God! (*Pause*) Will you say *you* did it?

*She stares at him, incredulously.*

MR E   (*in kitchen*) Everything alright in there?

## 23   The hall

*About 8 p.m. Again a frenzy of activity. (Perhaps the busiest period of all.) Voters, mostly in working clothes, are entering, registering, marking their ballots, putting them in the ballot box, or leaving.*

    *Mr Ellis, Mr Martin and Petula are at their desk, working non-stop. They're now much, much wearier, a little dishevelled and drawn.*

    *A man with one arm in a sling, and his other hand bandaged, is at the desk. He holds his polling card between his teeth – and is trying to say 'Can you take it, please?'*

MR E   Take his card, Miss Robinson, before he swallows it.

*She takes the card from his mouth and starts to check it against the register.*

MAN  Ta. (*He glances down at the register – it's badly stained, crumpled and sellotaped, but now dry*) Your paperwork's in a right state, isn't it?

MR E  It's suffering from exhaustion. Still, it's had a nice cup of coffee, a rest on the radiator and half a roll of sellotape. Which is more than *I* have. Been in the wars a bit yourself, I see.

MAN  You should've seen her husband.

MR E  Do you want me to mark your ballot paper for you?

MAN  Is it allowed?

MR M  Oh, it's obligatory. Paragraph 48 – physical incapacity, Jews voting on a Saturday, and illiterates.

*He smiles at Petula, hoping she's impressed. She ignores him, coldly.*

MR E  You'll have to tell me who you want to vote for, of course.

MAN  Well, none of them, by rights.

*He's interrupted by a voice from a loudspeaker in a car outside.*

LOUDSP  Today is polling day. Today is polling day. There are two hours left to vote. Vote Conservative.

MAN  (*to Mr Ellis*) Go on, then. Liberal.

LOUDSP  Vote for common sense. Vote Conservative.

MR E  Miss Robinson, tell the bobby to shut that bloody comedian up.

PETULA  (*getting up*) Righto.

MR M  (*rising*) Shall *I* go?

*She ignores him, nose in the air, and exits.*


**24  The hall (an hour or so later)**

*Mr Ellis, Petula and Mr Martin, all now even more tired, behind the desk. Voters are still busy voting.*

*A middle-aged woman, who has just been handed her ballot paper, hovers at the desk.*

WOMAN  Thank you. Um . . . what do I do now?

MR E  Just go to the booth over there.

WOMAN  (*pointing*) Over there?

MR E   Over there.

WOMAN   Where they are?

MR E   Where they are?

WOMAN   Righto. (*She stands, worried*) Then what?

MR E   Just mark your vote.

WOMAN   Righto. (*Stands a moment*) What do I put?

MR E   A cross.

WOMAN   I see. (*Pause*) Just, you know, a cross, like?

MR E   That's all.

WOMAN   Where?

MR E   Where what?

WOMAN   You said I'd to put a cross.

MER E   In one of those three spaces.

WOMAN   (*looks at ballot paper*) Oh, I see. Fair enough. (*Pause*) Which one?

MR E   Is it the first time you've voted?

WOMAN   No, I never miss.

MR E   Well, which candidate do you *want* to vote for?

WOMAN   Well, they're all the same, really, aren't they? None of them give a damn, deep down. Which do *you* think?

MR E   It's not for us to decide.

WOMAN   No . . . (*Pause*) Can you give us a hint?

MR M   Madam. In that booth, there's a notice for your guidance, with a sample ballot paper pinned underneath. Just read it.

WOMAN   Well, I hope it's more help than you lot.

*She starts for the booth. Mr Ellis sighs.*

MR E   God, I'm getting old.

PETULA   I think *I* am.

MR M   (*Suddenly, in alarm*) Oh, no!! (*They look at him*)

MR E   What?

*He is staring incredulously at the woman in the booth. They follow his gaze.*

MR M   She's putting her cross on the bloody sample!! (*He turns apologetically to Petula*) Sorry.

PETULA   What for?

MR M   Swearing.

PETULA   You can sing dirty songs if you like, I couldn't care less.

**25  The hall**

*One or two voters voting. Otherwise a quiet lull.*

*Mr Ellis and Petula seated at the desk, both now perilously near total exhaustion.*

*Now that she has a moment to herself, Petula's thoughts dwell on her day with Mr Martin.*

*Mr Ellis lights his pipe. He glances at her.*

MR E   Penny for them.

PETULA   (*sighing*) I'd be overcharging you.

MR E   Do you have a christian name, Miss Robinson?

PETULA   I can't remember, I don't think so. (*He smiles*)

MR E   Are you going to survive, do you think? I haven't seen you eat anything for about ten minutes.

PETULA   I had some wheatgerm and honey and a vitamin E. (*A silence*)

MR E   Let's hope Mr Martin feels better after his snooze. (*Looks at his watch*) He's had five minutes. We'll give him another five.

PETULA   He can have another five *years* for me!

MR E   Oh, I see. (*Puffs at his pipe*) Have you fallen out with him, then?

PETULA   I wouldn't touch him with a ten-foot ballot poll!

MR E   *Barge* pole.

PETULA   Mmm? Oh, yes, barge pole. Odd, really, I don't even like his face any more. It's getting uglier every minute.

MR E   It's getting tired, that's all. I know how it feels.

PETULA   He's such a . . . so pompous . . . full of himself. (*Mimicking Mr Martin*) 'Paragraph 25, Paragraph 89' – Paragraph . . . (*She tries to think of a swear word*) – pimple!

MR E   I was like that once. At *my* first election. Thought I knew it all. Mind you, I still do.

*A pause. Then . . .*

PETULA   (*quietly, almost tearfully*) It was him that spilt the coffee, you know, not me.

MR E   You said it was *you*.

PETULA   He wanted me to take the blame in case the whole poll was ruined. I could never forgive him for that.

MR E   You *did* take it, though!

PETULA   Only because I wanted to.

MR E   (*puzzled*) Eh?

PETULA   Well, he *let* me, didn't he! That's even worse. I could never forgive him for that even more.

*A voter enters and presents his card to Petula. She looks at it.*

PETULA   I'm afraid you've come to the wrong polling station. You want Conroy Street Junior School.

VOTER   Where's that?

PETULA   Conroy Street.

VOTER   Can't you slip me in here?

MR E   You're not on this register.

VOTER   (*snatching his card back*) Right cushy number you've got, haven't you?

*He lumbers off.*

MR E   (*to Petula*) I don't think I followed the logic of your last remark.

PETULA   You're not a woman. *Mrs* Ellis would.

MR E   Ah. (*Pause. Puffs on his pipe*) Anyway, he certainly seems a lot keener on *you*, now.

PETULA   Yes, that turns me off most of *all*. It did from the minute he started. (*She looks at him, troubled, sad*) I'm emotionally immature, aren't I? Mr Ellis?

*A voter enters and presents his card to Mr Ellis.*

VOTER   Who's winning?

MR E   (*searching the register*) Winning what?

VOTER   The election.

MR E   (*shrugs*) Who knows?

VOTER   You know what *I* do. Vote for one lot and bet five quid on the other. Either way I'm laughing.

MR E   (*giving him a stamped ballot paper*) Shows you.

*The voter goes to the booth.*

PETULA   Aren't I, Mr Ellis? Immature.

MR E   Miss Robinson. You've sat here all day in the middle of what's known as the most mature democracy the . . .

PETULA   I mean about boyfriends!

MR E   We weigh up the parties. They woo us. Lie to us. Give us the Oh-Be-Joyful. Promise us the moon. And we fall for one of them. And the minute we do – what do they do? Break their promises. And what do *we* do? Grumble, and flirt with the other lot at the Municipal Elections to make them jealous, and go through the whole rigmarole again. It's taken us centuries to get that far. It's taken you a day.

PETULA  I only want ... I don't know *what* I want.

MR E  That's right, love.


## 26  In the hall

*Petula and Mr Martin at the desk. A couple of voters on their way out.*

*Mr Martin is trying to summon up courage to make a date with Petula. She busies herself with whatever documents are on the desk to prove her obliviousness to his presence. Finally ...*

MR M  Miss Robinson?

PETULA  I can't offer you anything. I've eaten it all.

MR M  (*thrown*) What?

PETULA  What?

MR M  No, I was thinking of ... (*He steels himself*) When's the next NALGO dance?

PETULA  Why?

MR M  I was ... considering contemplating going.

PETULA  Good. Tell Sandra Tattersall.

*A young woman (Margaret Ridehalgh) enters and approaches the desk.*

MRS R  Evening.

PETULA  Good evening. (*She takes her polling card*) Thank you.

*Petula starts checking the register.*

MRS R  Working overtime?

PETULA  (*with a pinched smile at Mr Martin*) He is!

MRS R  (*puzzled*) Mmm?

*Mr Martin, aggrieved, hands her the stamped ballot paper.*

MR M  Thank you.

*A young man enters and approaches the desk (Barry Ridehalgh)*

MR R  How de do.

MR M  (*taking his card*) Thank you.

*As Mr Martin checks the register, Mr Ridehalgh waves at Mrs Ridehalgh in the booth. She waves back.*

MR M  Barry Ridehalgh?

MR R  Yep.

MR M  13, Whitley Crescent?

MR R  Yep.

MR M  You've already voted.

MR R  I've what??

MR M  You're already ticked off.

MR R  I've only just bloody walked in!!

MR M  I'm sorry, but your name's already ... (*He refers back to his register*) There's only a *Margaret* Ridehalgh of that address who hasn't yet vo ... (*He trails off as he realises the error*)

MR R  (*pointing to his wife in the booth*) *That's* Margaret Ridehalgh, sweetheart! I'm *Barry* Ridehalgh. She's voted, and I'm stood here like a bloody Christmas card!

MR M  Yes ... um ... I'm afraid we've ... um ... we've ticked you off instead of your wife.

PETULA  Oh, heck! I must have done it! I attended to Mrs ...

MR R  Tick *her* off then, give me my bit of paper and *I'll* go and vote!

MR M  I can't.

MR R  Why?

MR M  According to the rules you've already voted. (*He looks despairingly at Petula and gets his handbook out*)

MR R  But I haven't, have I, Little Noddy?

MR M  Hang on. You're allowed a tendered vote. That's different.

MR R  *How* different?

MR M  It doesn't go in the box. It's added later after the ...

*A sudden quick scuffle. Mr Ridehalgh leans forward and grabs him by the collar. Mr Martin tries to fight him off.*

PETULA  (*screaming*) Mr Ellis! Mr Ellis!

*Mr Ellis strolls out of the Committee Room, a half-full milk bottle in his hand.*

MR E  What the hell.

MR R  Are you in charge?

MR E  Are you assaulting my polling clerk?

MR R  With intent to maim.

MR E  Miss Robinson, get the policeman.

MR R  He won't let me bloody vote!! (*Releases him*)

MR M  I made a slight error, Mr Ellis. I ticked off his wife instead ...

PETULA  *I* did it, Mr Ellis!

MR E  Yes, alright.

PETULA  I did, honest! Mr Martin's only . . .

MR M  He's fully entitled to a tendered vote.

PETULA  It was with talking about the NALGO dance . . .

*Throughout, Mr Ellis has been examining the register, whistling softly to himself. They stand awaiting his verdict.*

MR E  OK. Just tick Margaret Ridehalgh off, and it all never happened.

*He stamps a ballot paper and gives it to Mr Ridehalgh.*

MR R  Bloody ta!

*He goes off to the booth.*

MR M  Which of us was right though, Mr Ellis?

MR E  Both of you, lad. As ever. (*He flops down in his chair, wearily. Takes a gulp of milk from his bottle*) By hell, I'm tired. (*Looks at this watch*) Fourteen hours gone, one to go. (*He sighs and leans back*) Lousiest time of the day, this. When you're old and grey . . . probably tomorrow, you'll look back on it as the longest hour of your life.

PETULA  (*suddenly*) Ssshhh! Shush a minute!

*Mr Ellis and Mr Martin look at her. She nods towards the booth. Mr and Mrs Ridehalgh are deep in whispered conversation.*

MR R  Go on, love.

MRS R  I want to vote for the *other* one.

MR R  I'll buy you a Mars Bar.

MRS R  No, Barry!

MR R  A tumble-twist rug. Just put a nice little cross on the . . .

MRS R  I said no!

*Cut back to Mr Martin, Mr Ellis and Petula.*

MR M  He's bribing her! Paragraph 79! Corrupt and Illegal Practices e.g. bribery, treating, undue influence and illegal payment!

MR E  (*looking the other way*) *I* can't hear anything!

PETULA  *I* can!

MR M  It's a criminal offence – punishable by law!

MR E  Only if the Presiding Officer hears it.

*Cut back to Mr and Mrs Ridehalgh.*

MR R  One of them cooking things you're always on about . . . go on . . .

MRS R  I want to vote for the *young* one.

MR R  You know, a sort of pan thing, with a draft name.

MRS R  A wok!

MR R  A wok!

MRS R  OK, then.

MR R  Good lass.

*They both mark their votes, Mr Ellis pretends to cock an ear.*

MR E  See . . . Can't hear a dicky-bird.

*He settles back with his eyes closed. Mr Martin sighs.*
*During this and the following exchange Mr and Mrs Ride-halgh put their papers in the box and exit.*

MR M  Mr Ellis?

MR E  (*wearily, eyes closed throughout*) Present.

MR M  Your wife.

MR E  My wife.

MR M  When she came in this morning.

MR E  When she came in this morning.

MR M  She told me about you never going to the Mayor's do after the count.

MR E  She tells everybody. I expected her to hire a loudspeaker.

MR M  You might enjoy it.

*Mr Ellis finally opens one eye, and fixes him with it.*

MR E  Do Morecambe and Wise know about you?

MR M  You *might*.

MR E  (*shakes his head and closes his eyes again*) No, no. Home. Bed. Sleep. Perchance not to bloody-well dream.

*A moment of peace, quiet and absolute stillness – suddenly shattered by a crashing noise at the door.*
*The three of them swivel round in alarm – to see a drunken man lurching in.*

DRUNK  Hey!!

MR E  Yes?

DRUNK  (*immediately launching into song*) 'Did you happen to see the most beautiful girl in the world? If you saw her, was she crying? Crying . . .'

MR M   Oh, my God.

DRUNK   Hey!! (*A woman has entered to vote. He at once directs the next verse to her*) (*Singing*) 'If you happen to see the most beautiful girl in the world, tell her I'm sorry. Sorry . . .'

WOMAN   (*to Mr Ellis*) I'll come back when you're not so busy.

*She exists hastily. The drunk turns back to the others.*

DRUNK   (*singing*) 'I love you, love, and only you, love, I love you, love me, oh yeah.'

*Mr Ellis has come round the desk to calm him.*

MR E   Alright, then, are we, mate?

*The drunk put his arm round Mr Ellis's shoulder and sings with deep feeling.*

DRUNK   (*singing*) 'Now solitaire's the only game in town, And every road I turn to turns me down, And by myself it's easy to pretend . . .'

MR E   Miss Robinson, a cup of black coffee.

MR M   Shouldn't we have him slung out?

MR E   Paragraph 73, laddie. If he knows why he's here, he's a right to vote. (*To the drunk*) Had a good time, then, have we, pal?

*Petula makes for the kitchen.*

DRUNK   Hello, sexy!

MR M   Shall I strike him?

*The drunk begins a short forward and backward dance – his arm still round Mr Ellis's shoulders.*

DRUNK   (*singing*) 'That's neat, that's neat, that's neat, that's neat, oh how I love your Tiger Beat! That's neat, that's . . .'

MR E   Can you answer some questions, Colonel?

*The drunk still singing, hands him his polling card.*

MR E   Good lad. (*Hands the card to Mr Martin*) Read him questions one and two from your bible. (*To the drunk*) Sssshh, a quiz for you.

MR M   (*reading from the handbook*) Are you the person registered in the Register of Parliamentary Electors for this election as follows . . . (*He checks the card against the register*) Magna Carta . . . Sorry, *Matthew* Carter, 88 Chapel Street?

DRUNK   Guilty, your Honour!

MR E  (*to Mr Martin*) Count that as affirmative. Question two.

MR M  (*reading from the handbook*) Have you already voted in this election, otherwise than as a proxy for some other person?

DRUNK  Have I hell!

MR  That sounds like a negative. Stamp the ballot paper.

*The drunk has now launched into 'I'd like to teach the world to sing in perfect harmony'.*
*Mr Martin hands him the stamped ballot paper.*

MR E  This, way, Squire.

*Arms round each other's shoulder, Mr Ellis leads him to the booth, leaves him there, and returns, wearily, to the desk.*

*Petula bustles out of the kitchen, with a mug of coffee. She glances at the drunk (still singing) and screams in horror dropping the coffee to the floor. Mr Ellis and Mr Martin look at her. She's staring, eyes popping, at the booth. They follow her eyes. On the floor, between the drunk's feet is a trickle of liquid.*

*Mr Ellis races frantically to the booth. A momentary scuffle. Mr Ellis turns round to face them, holding a half-empty bottle of beer.*

*He pants and gulps for a moment from his efforts, then – flatly –*

MR E  It's beer. He spilt his beer. He only spilt his beer. It's beer.


## 27  The hall (some time later)

*Petula is mopping up the spilt beer with a bucket and mop. She is very, very tired. Mr Martin and Mr Ellis are slumped at the desk.*

*Mr Ellis, chin on chest, is fighting to keep himself from nodding off.*

*Mr Martin sighs heavily.*

MR M  I think *I* can feel it now, Miss Robinson.

PETULA  (*past caring*) Feel what?

MR M  My head a long way from my body. (*He looks at his watch, then, flatly*) Two minutes to ten. Two minutes to go. Two minutes left, Mr Ellis.

*Mr Ellis lifts up his head.*

MR E  (*flatly*) Mr Martin . . . Miss Robinson . . . I think I've come to a decision. (*They look at him*) I'm hanging up my ballot-box. I think I've had enough. My last two minutes as a Presiding Officer. The next election can manage without me. The Queen won't mind.

PETULA   Aaahh . . . Why though?

MR E   Oh, a million reasons, I think. (*Pause*) It was probably Mr Carter, Inebriate of this Parish, that finally did it.

MR M   He was no worse than a few hundred others really. Pinching the pencils. Voting for the wrong ones. Voting for nobody. Insulting us. Throwing ballot papers out of the window. Sticking fag-ends in the ballot box.

*Mr Ellis smiles, wearily.*

MR E   By hell . . . *you've* changed. No, it wasn't spilling the beer that did it. The very opposite. It was because he *hadn't* done what we *thought* he'd done.

MR M   Eh???

MR E   If you follow my meaning.

MR M   No, I *don't*.

MR E   You will. One day. (*He looks at his watch*) Six, five, four, three . . . OK Miss Robinson. Stand by for the most beautiful sentence in the language: go and lock the door.

PETULA   (*with sighs and smiles*) Wow!

MR M   (*leaning back*) Hallelujah!!

*Petula goes to lock the door. Just as she's about to lock it, a woman pops her head round.*

WOMAN   Not too late, am I?

*They look at her, bleary-eyed. The town hall clock begins to chime ten o'clock.*

MR E   You made it by a second, Missus . . .

WOMAN   (*brightly*) Oh good!

MR E   *Now* lock the door, Miss Robinson.

*As Petula starts closing the door, it's being pushed open again from the other side.*
    *Puzzled, she opens the door.*

### 28 The foyer

*Terry Elliott, the bit of rough Petula gave the glad-eye to earlier, is
lounging against the wall, pushing the door open with his foot. Petula
pops her head round the door from the inside.*

TERRY   (*grinning*) How do, darling.

PETULA   Oh!

TERRY   Finished work?

PETULA   Pardon?

TERRY   You knock off at ten, don't you? 'Knock-off' – get it? (*He
winks*)

PETULA   (*scared*) Pardon?

TERRY   Come on. I'll see you home. (*He winks again*)

PETULA   I can't!

TERRY   Can't what?

PETULA   I'm not going home! I live here!

TERRY   Now listen, scrubber. No tart mucks *me* about and . . .

MR E   Miss Robinson! That door must be *locked*.

PETULA   Yes, Mr . . . El . . . father. (*To Terry*) That's my father. I'm
going home with him.

*She closes the door on him and locks it.*


### 29 The hall

*The woman is in the booth. Petula returns from the door.*

PETULA   Would you believe it! It was that boy! He asked me . . .

MR E   Yes, we heard.

MR M   (*suddenly blurting out*) Would you come home with *me*, Miss
Robinson?

PETULA   What??

*Mr Martin is embarrassed at Mr Ellis's presence.*
    *Mr Ellis goes over to the other desk, pretending to be suddenly
absorbed in the documents on it.*
    *Mr Martin and Petula face each other shyly.*

MR M   (*haltingly, nervously*) Just for some supper. A banana or
something. You'll be quite safe. My mother'll be in. We can
watch the results coming through and the swingometer. It'll
be terrific.

WOMAN   (*from the booth*) Sorry to keep you waiting.

MR E   Yes, madam. (*To Mr Martin and Petula*) Get your coats on.

*They exit to kitchen (or committee room) – Petula thoughtful, Mr Martin waiting for her reply.*

MR E  You take your time, love. You never know – it may turn out to be the casting vote.

WOMAN  (*horrified*) Oh, don't say that! (*Mr Ellis realises he shouldn't have*) Now I'll never be able to ... (*Suddenly*) I know! (*She turns decisively to mark her paper, then stops*) Or perhaps I'd better ... yes! (*She's about to mark her paper then stops again*) Hang on, though ... (*Sighs*) Oh, I don't know ... Sometimes I think ... and then I think ... (*Mr Martin and Petula return with their coats, bag, briefcase, crash helmet, and belongings*) Or should I ... That's it! ... No, I'll ... or should I ...? (*Impatient*) Oh, tinker, tailor, soldier, sailor ... (*suddenly*) I know! I'll shut my eyes.

*She jabs the ballot paper with the pencil like a pin.*
*Mr Ellis, Mr Martin and Petula look at each other. The final irony.*
*She folds her paper and puts it in the box.*

WOMAN  (*exiting*) Aren't I a terror! Goodnight.
MR E  Sleep tight.

*He follows her to the door, opens it for her. She exits. He locks it again.*
*Mr Martin and Petula are putting their coats on.*

MR E  And now, children, at last, at last, the ballot is closed.

*He takes the key from his pocket and locks the ballots box.*

MR M  Hallelu ... (*He stops abruptly, horror striken*) Oh, my God!!!
PETULA  What?
MR M  Oh, my God.
MR E  What?
MR M  I forgot to vote!!

*Mr Ellis manages to control a smile. Petula is filled with dismay, sympathy – and tenderness.*

MR M  (*heartbroken*) I forgot to vote. Me. I've thought of nothing else for ... It's the whole point of ... I've been here fifteen bloody hours and I forgot to vote! It's all been for nothing.
PETULA  Not nothing! If it wasn't for you, *no* one could have voted, could they, Mr Ellis?
MR M  (*half to himself*) Nothing.

PETULA  Mr Martin. I'd *like* to come home with you. I accept. Thank
you.

MR M  (*looking at her and smiling*) Honest?

PETULA  (*smiling back*) You mustn't feel rotten.

MR M  No. Always next time. (*Turns to Mr Ellis*) Should we wait for
you? You've tons of stuff to do yet.

MR E  No, no. Off you go.

R M  You've the ballot box to seal, and the statements to fill in,
and the accounts, and the lists, and all the packets to . . .

MR E  Mr Martin. I know what I have to do. Now clear off, the pair
of you, before you fall over.

*They go to the door. We hear night atmosphere sounds, a distant train,
etc.*

PETULA  Goodnight, Mr Ellis. Don't forget to put the key back under
the mat.

MR E  No. (*He smiles at them both*) Goodnight, Miss Robinson.

MR M  Goodnight, Mr Ellis.

MR E  Goodnight, Mr Martin. (*They open the door*) Hey. (*They turn*)
Thanks. You did alright.

*Perhaps the highest compliment they could hope for. They smile
acknowledgement, very, very sleepily, and exit. Mr Ellis stands for a
moment. All is now very quiet. He sighs and goes to the committee
room.*

### 30 The committee room

*Mr Ellis enters, goes to the 'phone and dials.*

MR E  (*into phone*) Mayor's Parlour, please. Ta. (*Pause*) Mrs
Bainbridge? Hello, love, Mr Ellis here, Polling Station
Number Four. Just to let you know Mrs Ellis and I will be
coming to the do tonight (*Pause*) Yes, it is a bit of a
precedent. (*Pause*) Just that this year, I thought I'd like to.
Pleasure. (*Pause*) Mushroom vol-au-vents? (*Pained*) Super.

### 31 Outside the hall (night)

*A dustcart rolls up and stops outside. A dustman gets out of the cab,
and makes his way to the entrance of the hall.*

## 32  The hall

*Mr Ellis is at his desk, smoking his pipe.*

*Before him, on the desk, is the sealed ballot box and the huge, bulging envelope containing all the documents.*

*A knock at the door. Mr Ellis drags himself to the door and opens it. The dustman is there.*

DUSTMAN  Got your ballot-box, flower?

MR E  It's all yours, sir.

*The dustman enters, picks up the box and envelope and starts to exit.*

DUSTMAN  Want a lift to the Town Hall?

MR E  The walk'll do me good.

*The dustman exits. Mr Ellis gives the silent, battle-scarred room one last glance of mixed feelings, then turns the lights out, and exits.*

## 33  The hall (night)

*As Mr Ellis emerges, we see a car drive up and stop.*

MRS E  Ooh – ooh! I've brought the car back!

*She's in the driving seat. He goes over to it, and starts to get in.*

## 34  Inside the car

MR E  Turn left at Market Street. We're going to the Town Hall.

MRS E  What??

MR E  I've decided.

MRS E  I don't believe it!

MR E  Well, we are.

MRS E  We're going straight home. *I* decided.

MR E  Eh??

MRS E  You were right. I'm a selfish woman.

MR E  I was wrong, Wendy! We're going.

MRS E  Home.

MR E  To the Town Hall!

MRS E  I've got your dinner in the oven.

MR E  I've told Mrs Bainbridge!

MRS E  I've got you a Chinese meal from the take-away. It's ages since you'd had Chinese.

*As they argue, the camera moves to show them from the front of the car. The windscreen wipers are going to and fro. They are arguing in time with the movement of the windscreen wipers.*

MR E  I was thinking of you.

MRS E  You weren't. I'm not even dressed for it!

MR E  I'm not bandying words with you after a hard day's . . .

MRS E  It's you that starts.

MR E  It isn't.

MRS E  Yes, it is.

*The music fades up and drowns their argument as we watch the wipers move to and fro.*

# Points for Discussion and Suggestions for Writing

## P'tang, Yang, Kipperbang

1 The first scene is a perfect introduction to the play. See if you can analyse what Jack Rosenthal achieves in it. What do you think of the use of John Arlott's commentary to 'reflect' the real action throughout the play?

2 Is Alan 'a child of his times'? Do you think that the agonies Alan suffers in the play are felt by teenagers today? Consider first his dream to save England's cricketing honour in the match against Bradman's Australians. TV programmes like 'Jim'll Fix It' are proof that we all have similar fantasies. Describe yours – as it might happen.

3 Consider Alan's fantasies about Ann. Why, when he is aware of his sexuality, does he want only to kiss her? Look at some of his speeches on kissing (scene 14, scene 30). How is he different from his friends?

4 What are Alan's feelings about Tommy? What does the headmaster mean when, telling Miss Land about Tommy's arrest, he adds, 'The dichotomy of Appearance and Reality again'? Why is this so ironic here? Write the letter Alan might send Tommy in prison. Look at Alan's speeches on peace and war first (scene 14).

5 'Filth! Beasts of the Field', shouts Miss Land when she witnesses Eunice being 'pressed' by Alan. Do such 'double standards' exist today about teenage sexual awareness? What do you think of Eunice? And of Miss Land? Should sexual expression ever be termed 'filth'? In what way do the affairs of the three adults form a contrast to the three adolescents?

6 The compliments Alan gives Ann, especially in scene 74, are utterly sincere – and nearly all physical. What is Ann like? Why is Alan's sort of idealisation an important 'phase' in our relationship with the 'opposite sex'? This play opened a TV series on Channel 4 called 'First Love'. Write

a play or story with that title, perhaps based on your own experience.

7 When Alan tells Ann, 'I breathe in on purpose to smell your skin', she replies, 'It's only Yardley's'. Why is this both funny and sad? Why do we often find it embarrassing to accept compliments gracefully? Write Ann's diary, covering the events of the play from her point of view.

8 'Would you like to kiss me now?'

'It's too late, Ann.'

Why does Ann want Alan to kiss her at the end? Why didn't he in the school play?

We can probably all find a time in our lives when, like Alan 'who went to the wicket a boy, and came back a man', we grew up a little – or a lot. It's usually both painful and positive to realise some truth about ourselves. What did Alan discover here? Can you write about a similar experience?

9 Despite John Arlott's final commentary of triumph, Rosenthal concludes the play with the two worksmen muttering:

'He'll be starting shaving next.'

'Then spend the rest of his life trying to stop the bleeding.'

Look at the other times the workmen appear. Did you notice how they form a second 'chorus' to Arlott, but that their tone is different? Why did Rosenthal include them?

10 'P'tang Yang Kipperbang uuh', 'chippiness lumpdom', 'paternal jobosity' ... 'Drivel', says Ann, 'Long, stupid words that don't mean anything.' To which Alan replies, 'It's only in fun. It's a joke.'

What do you think? And why do the teenagers – even Ann and Geoffrey – use such expressions? Are there similar ones today?

We now tend to 'borrow' a lot of expressions from the media – rather as Shaz and Abbo mock Geoffrey's running in 'terminology' from the Goon Show (scene 31). Can you write down similar popular examples, past and present?

11 Even if the opening did not offer the information that the play is set in 1948, what clues give you some idea of the date? What has changed more: people's attitudes or the environment we live in?

Choose a scene, and work out what scenery, clothes and

props would be required to make it 'authentic'. You could find some photographs from older relatives and talk to them of their memories of the time.

12 What do you think of the school life portrayed? How has education changed since then? You might like to do some research on this. If you were to write a play in years to come, using your present school days as background, what aspects do you imagine would have 'historical interest'?

13 Did you become aware of the implication of the names 'Miss Land' and 'Tommy'? Look at some of their conversations, especially in scene 26 and some of Alan's prophesies, and decide what Jack Rosenthal is saying in a wider context.

14 What is the effect of intertwining the scenes of the school play with the arrival of the police? Look for other places in the play where a similar juxtaposition of scenes is successful.

15 Write a review of the school play as it might appear in that school magazine. Or write a review of 'P'tang, Yang, Kipperbang' itself.

16 There are some highly entertaining scenes, and especially dialogues, in the play. Which did you find particularly amusing ... and why? Some of them are rather 'bitter-sweet', like the time Alan thinks Ann is smiling at him in the dining room. Find others and analyse the effect of Jack Rosenthal's writing like this.


## Polly, Put the Kettle On

1 'Five months I've had it! Swearing, arguing, everybody against me! We're here now ... and it's lovely ... and we're happy ...' See if you can script or improvise some of the arguments that Polly had with Christine and Warren. What part would Duggie have played?

2 'A white wedding', sighs Polly at the end. 'Church ... everything. Respectable married woman now ... No one can take that away. Photos and a write-up and dancing ... and singing ... Well, it's all happy memories, isn't it?'

Why do people get married? Would it worry you if you learnt that your parents hadn't married? Do you agree with Christine that her wedding is 'hypocrisy, the whole thing?'

What do you think a wedding should be like? You might like to conduct a survey amongst your married friends and relations to find out if weddings differ much, and if they have happy memories of their own. See if you can find out why some of the traditions and 'trappings' surrounding a marriage have come about – like confetti and bridesmaids.

3 Write the speech that Polly would have preferred Warren to give. Or produce the write-up in the local paper that Polly goes on about.

4 Did you notice Polly's obsession with having everything and everybody photographed? Look back through the play, and write the description that the photographer would give of the wedding later to his mates.

5 When Christine looks at the photo of Polly and Duggie outside Newcastle Register Office, she wonders, 'It can't all have been because of this, can it?' To what extent is she right?

6 'We'll be like my mum and dad.' Look at page 89 and decide whether you agree with Christine's prediction about her future with Warren. Will she, for instance, want a similar wedding for her daughter? What about your own future? Do you imagine you'll repeat your parents' lifestyle? Consider the lives of any married brothers and sisters before you answer that!

7 This play was one of a series entitled 'Seven Faces of Women'. In a sense this play might be called that too. What do you think of Rosenthal's title? When does Christine start to sympathise with Polly? How do our own feelings change in the course of the play towards Polly? See if you can pinpoint the exact moments this happens.

8 The scenes in the kitchen of the Co-op Hall are not essential to the main action of the play. But what would the play lose without them? You might like to script or improvise the scene which leads into our first encounter with the staff. (You'll need to re-read scene 4 first, and some of the later scenes for characterisation.)

9 There is one way in which our getting to know the kitchen team is vital. Would we appreciate Harry Chadwick's key role in the play without going 'below stairs'? Look at the final comments he makes to Duggie. Why is this a particularly masterful piece of writing?

10 'A good time was had by all'. The wedding guests would

probably be horrified that their antics could cause such amusement. What are your own memories of weddings you've attended? You might like to write a description, or put together a dramatisation, based on your experience.

11 Think about different forms of humour: slapstick, situation comedy, sick jokes, satire, visual or verbal humour, and find examples of each in the play.

## Well, Thank You, Thursday

1 This play was one of a series entitled 'Red Letter Day'. In what way does the play 'fit the bill'? Describe a red-letter day in your life; or take the same title to write a play or short story.

2 Let's consider the 'link person' first: deputy registrar, Miss Shepherd. What sort of person would you cast for her part if you were directing the play?

3 When Miss Shepherd's desk has not arrived, she recognises, 'It's probably the very least heartbreaking thing in the world. The least important. The least anything. And it's all I think about.' Why has a new desk taken on such significance?

4 Now look again at the conversation Miss Shepherd and Jenny have after Mr Patel's visit (scene 16). It points out that we all have our pre-occupations and 'funny little ways'. Choose a friend or relation and write about hers/his. Why is it easier for 'outsiders' to laugh at them? Imagine you are one of your parents, and describe your *own* most annoying habits!

5 Barry and Glenda have a 'problem' which, Miss Shepherd reveals, is very common. What is her 'long-practised con-trick'? And why does it back-fire? Are first names important? Ask your parents if they had any difficulty choosing your name. Do you like it?

6 Outside the clinic (scene 13), Glenda meets a baby Jason, and 'there are two other Jasons in there'. Is there a fashion in names? Why do you think *The Times* newspaper produces a 'top ten' list of the most popular names in their birth announcement column?

What about name-associations? Glenda remarks, 'I used to know a Damion at the hairdressers. His eyes were terribly close together.' Is it possible to avoid doing this?

And what about the 'pet names' Glenda and Barry give their baby? If you dare, reveal similar names in your family! Do they have to be ridiculous?

7 'Tomorrow morning,' says Liz to Stan when we first meet them, 'we'll be husband and wife ...' 'Which', points out the direction note, 'is precisely what has been worrying them both sick all night long.' Why are they so anxious? Describe an occasion when you felt equally nervous. Is it worth 'getting into such a state'?

8 Compare this wedding with Christine and Warren's in *Polly Put the Kettle On*. Which would you prefer, and why? Give the toast that Mike will make to Stan and Liz later that evening.

9 Perhaps the worst *faux-pas* made by Mick is when he asks Mr Crabtree, 'Your blushing bride? Done a bunk has she?' There are innumerable other hilarious 'one-liners' in the play. Which is your favourite, and why?

10 When Mr Crabtree explains that his wife 'has passed away this morning, official', he adds: 'Merciful release, really'. Look back through the play and write the description that Jack Rosenthal must have had in his mind when he invented Clara. Will Mr. Crabtree mourn or miss her?

11 Consider his comment to Miss Shepherd after the formalities are over: 'You'd think there'd be more to it after all them years ...' Do you think that society does enough to mark a death? What is, and what could be done? If you can, write about your experience of someone dying. You might like first to discuss why this is such a difficult task.

12 Have a look at the 'batch, match and dispatch' announcements in different newspapers. Then write the three that might have appeared after this play. (In the case of Glenda and Barry, any announcement would probably have been placed soon after the birth.)

13 Christian churches mark a baby's birth with a christening or baptism; Jewish families may have a circumcision ceremony. For weddings and funerals, society has devised civil ceremonies similar to religious ones. It might be interesting to make a comparison of the language and concepts used in each case. But so far there is no civil celebration to note a baby's entry into society. What ceremony would you suggest?

14 At the end of the play, Miss Shepherd 'surveys her desk,

uneasy at a growing sense of anti-climax, of depression. A feeling of flatness she can't explain.' Can you explain it? Compare her reaction to Alan's (in *P'tang, Yang, Kipperbang*) when Ann invites him to kiss her at the end. What did you feel when Mr. Crabtree stuck his chewing gum 'on the underside of the new desk'? Now look at the very last line of the play: how would you as director ask Dan to say it?

15 In a sense this play is about 'a day in the life of a Registrar'. You might like to take another building, and, dividing your class into groups, devise a similar dramatisation. Discuss first the way Jack Rosenthal has constructed his play; his arrangement of his scenes and characters might add to the success of your play.

## Mr Ellis Versus the People

1 'Right cushy number you've got, haven't you?' a voter comments late in the day to the polling clerks. Would you agree? Describe, for someone interested in the job, the sort of day he or she would experience.

2 'Government by the people for the people...' It's very easy, while enjoying the play, to forget the actual reason for an election, or in this case, a parliamentary bye-election. What do you think is Jack Rosenthal's serious intention in writing this play? And why did he write it as a comedy? See if you can find out about elections in other countries, and describe similar 'minor problems' at their polling stations.

3 Express your opinions (perhaps in a class debate) on these statements:
'We get the governments we deserve ...' (page 160)
'And something else you'll learn before the day's out – governments get the *electorate* they deserve...' (page 161)
'We weigh up the parties. They woo us ... And we fall for one of them. And the minute we do – what do they do? Break their promises. And what do *we* do? Grumble, and flirt with the other lot at the Municipal Elections to make them jealous, and go through the whole rigmarole again ...' (page 179)
'We're supposed to be the most politically sophisticated society in the world ...' (page 168)

4 It is in fact only in scene 7 that we realise play is going to be

set in a polling station. What then do the opening scenes establish?

5 As with *Well, Thank you, Thursday*, our interest is held as much by the occasion and events of the day, as by the individuals who reveal lives beyond their official roles. At the end of the play Mr Ellis says to Mr Martin, 'By hell, you've changed.' In what way is this comment true of all the main characters?

6 'I don't know what I want', sighs Petula. Write the letter she might have sent to an 'agony aunt' before the play. Then give an account of why her feelings towards Mr Martin vacillate during the day. Explain, for instance, her anger in scene 25.

7 What do you think of Mr Martin? Can you compare our responses to him to the way we feel for Polly during *Polly Put the Kettle On*? How true to life is his 'conversion' to showing interest in Petula?

8 Compare the two descriptions we are given of the mayor's election night party (scenes 21 and 22). Then write out the one Mr Ellis would give. See if you can find a similar function (perhaps school sports day) and give three contrasting reviews or previews of it.

9 There's a policeman at the door we're told, but his presence is never required, though Mr Ridelagh and the drunk cause some anxious moments for the polling clerks. Why do you think there is no scene depicting a violent act in this play – or any of the others in this volume? Compare Jack Rosenthal's approach to other TV playwrights.

10 As you have probably come to expect, there are some hilarious scenes and lines in the play. Explain why a selection of them are so amusing.

## General Questions

1 Look again at Jack Rosenthal's introduction to this volume, and then find moments in the plays where a 'character never actually listens to the others'.

2 All the lonely people ... Where do you think Jack Rosenthal most succeeds in his aims 'to make people aware of the pain of loneliness in other'?

3 Did you notice that our laughter in these plays is always *with*, never *at* the characters? Do you agree that 'comedy is

the best way to learn the truth about ourselves'? Think of other plays you know. Did you identify with any of the characters in Jack Rosenthal's plays? And did any particular situations or scenes make you aware how easy it is to accept the people we meet at face value only?

4 Jack Rosenthal says he likes to include the 'seven deadly sins' in his plays. See if you can match a character to each. Which character would you most like to play, and why?

5 Jack Rosenthal delights in letting the audience share a moment with him, unbeknown to the characters. Take one from these plays and analyse why it is successful.

6 What do you think Jack Rosenthal learnt about writing plays when writing episodes for Coronation Street? If you were told that he is preparing to write a play about moving house, focussing on a removal firm's day, what would you expect to see?

7 What short of research would Jack Rosenthal have had to undertake to prepare for these plays? Choose one and make a list of the people he might have consulted.

8 You might like to write a letter to Jack Rosenthal to give your views of these plays, or others of his that you have seen on television. Letters can be sent c/o

Longman Imprint Books
   Longman House
   Burnt Mill
   Harlow
   Essex
   CM20 2JE

# Note on the Author

Jack Rosenthal was born in Manchester in 1931. His father, Sam, was a factory-worker making mackintosh raincoats; a fanatical lover of all sports, he was opening batsman for an amateur cricket team called 'Red Rose' (despite being a Yorkshireman). Jack's mother Leah (nicknamed Lakey) was a machinist in a raincoat factory; an avid lover of gardening and cooking, her 'real-life dialogue was heaven-sent to a budding writer'. Two people of markedly opposite characteristics, Jack feels very much the child of them both.

He was educated at Colne Grammar School and Sheffield University, where he read English. After National Service in the Navy, he joined the promotion department of Granada Television in 1956, and after a spell in advertising went on, as he describes in the introduction, to write some 150 scripts for *Coronation Street*.

Scripts for other drama and comedy series followed, including 'That Was the Week That Was'. He originated three comedy series of his own: 'The Dustbinmen', 'The Lovers' – which received the Writer's Guild Best Comedy Series Award in 1971 – and 'Sadie It's Cold Outside'. He has now written over 24 TV plays, many of which have been nominated for and/or have won Best Play Awards, and now have the equivalent of classic status. *P'tang, Yang, Kipperbang* was nominated for the British Academy Best Play Award of 1983.

Jack Rosenthal's first award for a single play came in 1972 when *Another Sunday and Sweet F.A.* won the TV Critics' Circle Best Play of the Year Award and was included by the National Film Archive of the British Film Institute in their season of Television Drama 1959–1973; *The Evacuees* in 1975 won the International Emmy Best Play Award, British Academy Best Play Award, Broadcasting Press Guild Play Award and the Jerusalem Festival Special Award; *Bar Mitzvah Boy* won the British Academy Best Play Award and the Broadcasting Press Guild Best Play Award in 1976; and in 1977 *Spend, Spend, Spend* won the British Academy Best Play Award, and he received the British Academy Writer's Award and the Royal Television Society's Writer's Award. Many of these indicate the esteem held by fellow professionals and television critics for his writing. The last three plays mentioned have already been published by Penguin in *Three Award-Winning Television Plays*. *Another Sunday and Sweet F.A* is published by Paul Elek in *The Television Dramatist* (for details, see 'Further Reading').

Jack Rosenthal's reputation so far rests on his television and film work. He wrote the musical of *Bar Mitzvah Boy* in 1978 and then a stage play called *Smash!* which was an account of the making of the musical. With Barbra Streisand he wrote the screenplay of the feature film, *Yentl*, in 1982.

He lives in North London with his wife, actress Maureen Lipman, who has appeared in some of his plays, and their two children. He says his ambition is to write a play which pleases himself, the public, and the critics, all at the same time.

# A Note to Teachers

This is the second Longman Imprint Book devoted to the work of an individual television playwright (the other is *Still Waters and Other Plays* by Julia Jones). It marks an important development in the range of books brought to the classroom. At last writers whose plays are seen on television are being given the same recognition as those who write for the stage. Children, it has been established, watch over three hours of television every day, seven days a week. And no teacher will deny the influence carried by the attitudes and opinions expressed in all those programmes.

Yet, we, as teachers, do not seem to face the fact that far more of our pupils watch television than go to the theatre – or even read novels. English lessons offer encouragement to pupils to read good books and good stage plays, in order to discriminate between writing that has quality and writing that is common or garden. Do we do the same to help teenagers in their leisure hours select television programmes and video tapes with knowledge and expectations?

Perhaps too much attention is given in television drama to the 'star of the show'. And certainly, who would deny the pleasure of watching fine acting performances? But take a selection of newspaper reviews of last night's TV play, and see if the critics give any space to the dramatist . . . or to the craft involved in his or her creation.

The television playwright deserves as much attention – or more – as those (actors, directors) who take the script off the page. Television is his or her publisher. Even when written within a series, at least 50 per cent of the material is original and independent of any format. Few professional writers can afford to neglect writing episodes for series, which is why many of the scripts are very good indeed. But who stops to think why this week's episode was more interesting than last week's? Jack Rosenthal started his own script-writing with episodes of *Coronation Street* and admits he learnt most of the disciplines of television writing in that apprenticeship. There is no equivalent in other forms of literature to the sort of co-operative writing required in a television series. It presents a challenge to invent something original within the standard format, something pupils can be invited to try for themselves.

But Jack Rosenthal feels that the series frequently offers the very opposite of true drama. The audience is hardly affected by what happens in each episode. They don't really want to see their favourite characters doing anything out of the ordinary, and certainly don't want major changes in lifestyle or attitude to occur! For these reasons, Jack Rosenthal prefers the individual play. He likes the lifespan of a single event or issue and often writes within the classical unities. He says also that he needs the challenge of creating totally new characters who have something fresh to say ... even if, as he has admitted in the introduction to this book, the themes remain the same.

For the audience, of course, meeting these characters only once means taking a risk. In fact, just looking out for the single television play takes far more effort than turning on regularly at the same time each week. Teenagers probably need some guidance in using the daily papers and television magazines to find advance publicity about television plays. There is rarely a review to read first, a step that we can take before choosing a theatrical play to see. Knowing the names of television playwrights is a major step. Noting writers of stimulating plays means being able to select with discrimination in future. And, of course, discussion of why a particular play is successful never fails to create interest in the writer's next work.

We owe it to the television playwrights to give their potential audiences an insight into their craft ... and we owe it to those audiences to give them the expectation of pleasure or provocation.

# Wider Reading

## Television scripts

*Three Award Winning Television Plays: Barmitzvah Boy, The Evacuees* and *Spend, Spend, Spend* by Jack Rosenthal (Penguin).

*The Television Dramatist*, including *Another Sunday and Sweet F.A.* by Jack Rosenthal, selected and introduced by Robert Mullen (Paul Eleck).

*Conflicting Generations*, plays by John Hopkins, Paddy Chayefsky, David Turner, Ronald Eyre, and John Mortimer, collected by Michael Marland (Longman Imprint Books).

*Hancock's Half Hour* by Ray Galton and Alan Simpson (Evans).

*Joby, the television version*, by Stan Barstow (Blackie's Student Drama Series).

*Juliet Bravo*, five scripts from the BBC television series collected by Alison Leake (Longman Imprint Books).

*The Pressures of Life*, plays by Richard Harris, Barry Hines, Julia Jones, and Jeremy Seabrook, collected by Michael Marland (Longman Imprint Books).

*Scene Scripts*, seven plays from the BBC Schools series, including plays by Fay Weldon, Alan Plater, Bill Lyons, Ronald Eyre (Longman Imprint Books).

*Scene Scripts Two*, a further selection from the series, with plays by Leonard Kingston, Peter Terson, Colin Welland, Eric Paice, and Willy Russell (Longman Imprint Books).

*Scene Scripts Three*, another selection, with plays by David Hopkins, Jack Ronder, David Cook, and Leonard Kingston (Longman Imprint Books).

*Still Waters*, three television plays by Julia Jones, collected by. Alison Leake (Longman Imprint Books).

*Television Comedy Scripts*, five scripts from popular BBC comedy series, collected by Roy Blatchford (Longman Imprint Books).

*Z Cars*, four scripts from the long-running popular police series (Longman Imprint Books).

## Journals where discussion of television programmes and issues can be found

*The Listener*
*Sight and Sound*
*New Society*
*New Statesman*
*Radio Times*
*TV Times*

### Critical reading

*Television: technology and cultural form* by RAYMOND WILLIAMS (Fontana/Collins, 1974).
*Using the media* by DENIS MACSHANE (Pluto Press, 1979).
*Television violence and the adolescent boy* by W. A. BELSON (Teakfield, 1978).
*Report of the committee on the future of broadcasting* (1977) Cmnd. 6753 (HMSO) The 'Annan Report'.
*Children and television* edited by RAY BROWN (Cassell and Collier, 1976).
*The least worst television in the world* by MILTON SHULMAN (Barrie & Jenkins, 1973).
*The new priesthood: British television today* edited by Joan Bakewell, Nicholas Garnham (Allen Lane, 1970).
*BBC: public institution and private world* by Tom Burns (MacMillan, 1977).
*Writing for the BBC: a guide to writers on possible markets for their work* (BBC, 1983).
*Writing for television* by M. Hurke (Adam and Charles Black, 1981).
Open University Course Units
    Unit One: *Issues in the study of mass communications*
    Unit Ten: *Patterns of ownership*
    Unit Thirteen: *The media as definers of social reality*
    Published by The Open University.

# Acknowledgements

We are grateful to J. R. Moss of the City of London Polytechnic for assistance in compiling the bibliography.

We are grateful to the following for permission to reproduce photographs:

David Davidson Associates Ltd, pages 1, 58, 59, 60, 61 and cover; Granada Television Ltd, pages 107 and 147; London Weekend Television, page 63.

**Longman Imprint Books**
*General Editor:* Michael Marland CBE MA